TERRACE V. WHITE

PARENTING MEMOIR
From the Heart of a Single Father

Terrace V. White

Pearly Gates Publishing, LLC, Houston, Texas

PARENTING MEMOIR

Parenting Memoir:
From the Heart of a Single Father

Copyright © 2020
Terrace V. White

All Rights Reserved.
No portion of this publication may be reproduced, stored in an electronic system, or transmitted in any form or by any means (electronic, mechanical, photocopy, recording, or otherwise) without written permission from the author or publisher. Brief quotations may be used in literary reviews.

Print ISBN 13: 978-1-947445-96-3
Digital ISBN 13: 978-1-947445-97-0
Library of Congress Control Number: 2020911722

Disclaimer: The content is not intended to be a substitute for professional medical advice, diagnosis, or treatment. Always seek the advice of your physician or other qualified health provider with any questions you may have regarding a medical condition.

Scripture references marked NKJV (New King James Version) and NIV (New International Version) are used with permission from Zondervan via Biblegateway.com. Public Domain.

For information and bulk ordering, contact:
Pearly Gates Publishing, LLC
Angela Edwards, CEO & Chief Editorial Director
P.O. Box 62287
Houston, TX 77205
BestSeller@PearlyGatesPublishing.com

TERRACE V. WHITE

Dedication

This book is dedicated to the loving memories of my grandparents,

Arthur and Mary Parson,

for laying a solid foundation and being Godly examples.

I am missing both of you…

PARENTING MEMOIR

The following poem is dedicated to my mother, **Ruth White Turner**, in appreciation for her patience, kindness, wisdom, honesty, compassion, and faithfulness.

Amazing Ruth

Amazing Ruth! How sweet the sound
Of your endless love and prayers abound,
That help to save a wretch like me,
To bear fruit and be strong as an old oak tree.

'Twas His grace that anointed your lips;
It kept me safe, according to the script.
Oh, how precious are the gifts you give:
The hugs, the smiles, and lessons how to live.

Through the years and across the miles,
You saw my hurt and knew my many trials.
An encouraging word you never failed to release,
While your unconditional love abundantly increased.

The times we share are as fine as art,
For I know I was never forgotten from the very start.
The Lord's promises always kept us together
Because a mother's love is meant forever and ever.

Your compassion and kindness never told a lie.
Therefore, I will honor you even past our final good-bye.
I am always grateful and believe in truth.
You are forever in my heart, my Amazing Ruth!

Acknowledgments

I want to express my sincere love and gratitude to my children and my God!

Tangela, my firstborn and "Mini-Me": Your birth into this world softened my heart, gave me a purpose, taught me how to be a more responsible young man, and helped me become a better father. During my basketball playing years and beyond, you were my biggest cheerleader. Now, as you protect this great nation in which we live, our roles are reversed, and I could not be prouder of you!

Ebony, the "World Traveler": Thank you for being you, accepting me as a father figure, and sharing your perspectives. Your leadership qualities have been on display from an early age—from leading the neighborhood tea parties, to your chosen career path. Keep the faith! P.S. Real Dad!

Brandon, my only son, my "Dude": We have been riding since 1994 and are still going strong. Thank you for challenging my old ways of thinking and for displaying your most precious God-given talent: Art. Keep shining brightly and demanding that the world see you!

PARENTING MEMOIR

It has been a joy watching you all grow into productive Queens and King. I want you all to know that during the times we were physically apart as I served this country, not a day passed without seeing your smiling faces. I hope I have made you proud because I am immensely proud of you all. You have been a key source of my strength and motivation to share and embrace this journey as a single father. You will always have my love and support. I am looking forward to our continued growth and success!

To all my Aunts and Uncles who helped raise me: I am forever grateful for your love and support over the years. Prayerfully, I have made the family proud!

Last but not least, I thank my **Heavenly Father, my Lord and Savior,** for Your grace and mercy. I learn more and more about Your awesomeness every day. Regardless of the circumstances or how many times I slip up, You are always there for me with Your unconditional love. I will forever hold on to Your promises and praise Your Holy name. Thank You for not letting this dream fade away!

Preface

This book sat on the shelf of my mind and in the chambers of my heart for many years. I felt there was a need and a place for it but convinced myself I was not the one to tell and share the story.

First, I talked myself out of it. That was followed by doubt and no less than five false starts. After all, who would want to listen to me? What made my story and perspectives so different? Not being a so-called "expert" in child development and having no formal training in child psychology, I knew writing about parenting would be a tall order. Then I thought:

If not me, then who?

I had outstanding parenting examples from my grandparents. I have traveled the world and seen different parenting styles from other cultures as well. So, why not pursue this literary venture?

The subject matter continued to churn in my gut like handmade ice cream—and it would not go away. I noticed the challenges of parenthood became a regular topic in various conversations with friends and coworkers, kept showing up in movies, and even popped up in my dreams. To further thrust me into this assignment, while engaged in my personal Bible study one Saturday night, I read **Habakkuk 2:2 (NKJV):**

"Then the Lord answered me and said: "Write the vision and make it plain on tablets, that he may run who reads it."

After reading that verse, I was not sure where to start but knew I had received confirmation!

Excited about my clear direction, I toured three different bookstores as part of my research to see what kind of books were already on the market. In all three stores, the parenting books were sectioned by age groups (i.e., Pregnancy and Childbirth, Infants and Toddlers, School Age, Family and Relationships, and Child and Adolescent Challenges). I quickly noticed most of the books were written by women, including Elizabeth, Jenny, Carol, Brandi, Mary Beth, Rachel, Julie, and a host of others. I only saw a handful of parenting books written by men, with names like Robert, John, Michael, and Daniel. The discovery piqued my interest and caused me to dig a little deeper.

To ensure my mind was not playing tricks on me and that I was not overreacting, I decided to conduct an Internet search. After a few exhaustive hours of searching, I noticed none of the books on the shelves in the Parenting sections at three bookstores were written by African American authors and found very few on the Internet. I thought, *"How strange, considering there were over 1,000 books in that section in each store and many more available on the Internet!"*

In my mind, the question then became, *"What will I do with this eye-opening tidbit of information?"* I could either accept the parenting advice and stories written in those books **OR** turn a blind eye and choose another subject to write about.

As you can see, I decided to share a part of my story. Perhaps a look into my real-life parenting journey can help other single parents (not just fathers). If no one else wants to read about it, I am sure my children will get a kick out of it!

Parenting Memoir: From the Heart of a Single Father is the result of my heart's desire and best effort to share with you the highs and lows of single-parenting.

Introduction

Have you ever been excited to watch your favorite movie that features three or four of your favorite characters? You might have watched it several times, yet it still holds your attention just as it did on opening night. Each character has their own unique style, personality, and dynamic acting abilities. Each could have easily been tagged with the leading role. You welcome the supporting cast because you have seen them in cameo appearances in other movies. There are also a few extras you do not recognize but notice they keep appearing in the background. However, you do not mind their presence because they add an increased intensity to the overall plot. You are in a good place and deeply engaged as the movie hums along. Suddenly, one of the two main characters of the blockbuster movie unexpectedly dies.

That is exactly what happened to me! Well, not in the literal sense, but figuratively. The "blockbuster movie" was not a movie at all. It was my life—my reality—and I was tagged with the leading role.

You see, my comfortable and carefully planned life was humming along when I suddenly found myself cast into the leading role as a single father. I must admit: It was not an episode I auditioned for, but I bravely embraced it with little fear. The supporting cast included my children and all those people and organizations that continue to help turn down the temperature of parenting.

At the end of this life, hearing the words, *"Well done, My good and faithful servant,"* is yet to be written on the pages of my life. However, while I wear this temporary earth suit, I pledge to do my part as being the best father I can be.

Every single parent has their own unique story of how they became a single parent. Several of our stories are similar as we navigate the single life and its new parenting demands. Sadly, not all have a reliable support system or know where to get help when needed…*especially single fathers.*

Let us be honest here: Single women have filled the role of 'father' for **many** years. They have stepped up to the plate and done a remarkable job of leading the family when needed when the father is absent.

On the next few pages, I share a portion of my journey as a single parent—more specifically, as a single **father**. This is not a "How-To" book to teach you how to be a better parent or a better father. This book simply seeks to distill a father's wisdom to his children and encourage other single parents. It will give you a glimpse into my upbringing, career, parenting challenges, miscalculations, and the sense of resiliency encountered thus far as a single father. I also share some of my greatest joys of fatherhood and a few of my favorite Bible verses that helped me get through some rocky times. I am prayerful the carefully selected verses will have a similar impact on you and your situation as well.

Successful parenting cannot be reduced to a long list of dos and don'ts that is imposed on children or parents. Each day is different from yesterday. Each child is different from the other. Therefore, each opportunity presents unique ways for a parent to *teach, reach, and serve.*

Teaching provides a safe and sound foundation for your children to learn, make mistakes, and to grow.

Reaching includes constant communication with your children and breaking down tasks into their most basic form so that they can understand. (For inexperienced parents or a single parent, those tasks can seem overwhelming.)

Serving is ensuring that your children know you are always there for them, providing unconditional love no matter what.

How will you handle it all? Regardless of how you ended up on "Single-Parent Highway," somewhere along the journey, you will notice how things always come together when you let go and invite God to intervene.

It is my prayer that *Parenting Memoir: From the Heart of a Single Father* encourages not only my children, but all readers to trust the wisdom of God and their own parenting skills to build a better future for their family. As you read this book, hold it in your left hand to gain encouragement. In your right hand, hold and read the Holy Bible to gain knowledge of who God is, His character, and His desire to have a relationship with us. Read both together. Hopefully, doing so will help ease the rough areas you encounter on your parenting journey. Know that you will always have someone in your corner, cheering you on. **If I can do it, so can you!**

PARENTING MEMOIR

Table of Contents

Dedication vi
Amazing Ruth vii
Acknowledgments viii
Preface x
Introduction xiii
In the Beginning 1
My Gift to You 5
Opposite End of the Spectrum 6
Humble Beginning 15
The Root Cause 20
Family History 24
Fellowship 31
The Mission Statement 37
The Treasure of Fatherhood 40
God Will Provide 49
Medicine, Exercise, and Healthy Eating 58
Full Circle 71
It's All About the Money 77
"Poor Me" Syndrome 86
Trials Do Not Mean Failures 89
The Vow 93
Medical Emergencies Do Happen 98
Overcoming Misunderstood Behavior 104
Protect the Mind 110
Time Waits for No One 115

Dating	122
Fruit of My Labor	133
Life and Death	140
A Time to Re-Energize	151
The School Years	157
The ABCs of Life	168
The Hard Questions	173
Father's Day	178
A Call to Serve	183
My "Transitions"	203
Child Support	205
"The Talk"	213
Understand Me	222
Final Thoughts	225
About the Author	227
Appendix	229

PARENTING MEMOIR

In the Beginning

As the story is told in Genesis (the first Book of the Holy Bible), God created the heavens and the earth. Then, He went on to create everything in, under, and on them. There was light, grass, fruit trees, great living creatures, and eventually, man—whom He created in His own image. Both male and female were blessed and were told to *"be fruitful and multiply,"* among many other things. Reading that story got me to thinking about the miracle of life and just how precious it is.

The gestation period for a human is roughly nine months divided into three trimesters. During that time, another human is developed and grows inside the mother's womb. When you really think about it, isn't that a miracle within itself? Another thing that is occurring during the same time is the building of an unbreakable bond between baby and mother. While the father will have his time to build a strong bond, it is quite different and occurs much later in the process than the motherly bond. Although I was actively involved during the entire pregnancies and births of my children (including cutting their umbilical cords), it does not compare to the bond built early on between mother and child.

Over the years, I have had the privilege of smelling the fresh country air of England, feeling the unbearable heat of the East African coast, viewing a 50-foot table set with China made from pure gold that is fit for a king in Austria, and playing with the most extreme high-tech gadgets in Japan before their release in the United States. I have witnessed nightly eruptions of Mount Edna in Italy, taken postcard-perfect pictures of the German snow-covered mountain villages, seen one of the world's largest Mosques in Turkey, stood in awe at the amazing ice sculptures and northern lights of Alaska, and smelled the aroma of thousands of fresh flowers in Hawaii. I have tasted the fresh spring Colorado mountain water, felt the radiant sun of the Arizona western desert, playfully counted the endless raindrops in Georgia, and withstood the hurricane-force winds in Virginia. Those diverse and amazing experiences took me to the highest highs and the lowest lows.

Although I have seen and felt those magnificent wonders, **none** of them compares to the first time I laid my eyes on each of my children.

PARENTING MEMOIR

In the Fall of 2007, I experienced one of my many visions. I remember seeing a scene set in a small two-bedroom house that was filled with a modest amount of furniture and lots of family photos. The only noise I could hear was a constant "tick" coming from the stuck second hand of an old clock that had been passed down for three generations (in the past, it amazingly kept a more accurate time than any digital clock I have ever owned). A bright blinking light illuminated the small black molies, multicolored guppies, and angelfish as they darted in and out of the prepositioned plants and logs in the aquarium. The sunlight peeping through the window also pushed its way through the two-inch crack of the door to the master bedroom.

I recall proceeding with caution, being mindful not to disturb the picture-perfect scene of what I was witnessing: the sight of a pregnant mother enjoying her alone time with her unborn child. Not a word was spoken. Only the deafening silence and the perfect peace that only God can give—and, of course, lots and lots of smiles of joy—filled the room. I stood there watching and admiring the scene for a few minutes…although it seemed more like two hours. I remember selfishly thinking, *"I want to be a part of that encounter,"* but I knew it was a bonding setting only a mother could experience.

As I slowly backed away from the door, I sat quietly for the next couple of minutes. I needed to fully capture and decipher the vision and unique relationship I had just witnessed between mother and child. That came by way of a short poem titled "My Gift to You," which is shared on the following page.

PARENTING MEMOIR

My Gift to You
© 2007 Terrace V. White

Thirty-nine weeks in total darkness,
Held ever so tight in the depth of the belly.
So close, yet so far…
Your hands caress our skin,
Calmly taming morning sickness one stroke at a time.
Hours of staring in the mirror as our bodies grow,
Snickering at the untold secrets only known to the two of us.
Our eyes finally meet for the very first time.
A new, mystified beginning — always inseparable.
Divine intervention has come to pass.
Welcome to this world!
My gift to you is life, my child!
My gift to you is unconditional love, Mother!

Opposite End of the Spectrum

The vision described in the previous chapter may sound peaceful, tranquil, and innocent, but the opposite end of the spectrum can look entirely different.

A child's initial entry into this world, upbringing, and overall life may be chaotic and filled with uncertainty and guilt. Imagine a scene from the same scenario when the father backs out and decides to leave the children behind. You may hear children's cries that say:

"Don't leave, daddy!"

"I'll be good, daddy!"

"Daddy, please don't go!"

"What did I do, daddy?"

I am not sure if you have ever heard those words bellowed from deep down in the belly of a child, but just the **thought** of saying them can be devastating to a child.

Sadly, they are the words and thoughts of young, distraught children in many households across the world who are trying to get their father not to leave home or (more specifically) not to leave them behind. They are the words that often lead to emotional destruction or a slow, downward spiral of the mind of a child.

Those instances of parent abandonment are not best-selling Hollywood scripts. Rather, they are the reality of countless homes. However, it does not have to be that way.

According to the Custodial Mothers and Fathers and Their Child Support Report released by the U.S. Census Bureau, there were approximately 13.6 million single or custodial parents in the United States in 2016, and those parents were responsible for raising 22.4 million children. The report highlighted that the typical single parent is a gainfully employed woman raising one child from the absent parent, while over 46% have two or more children living with them. Those numbers give a snapshot, but they do not tell the real story behind the challenges of single-parenthood.

Unfortunately, there are too many negative statistics available that highlight what happens when the father or father figure is not present in the home. The father's absence can affect his children in various ways, to include:

- Youth suicide
- Runaways
- Homelessness
- Behavior disorders
- Anger issues
- School dropouts
- Early fatherhood
- Teenage pregnancy
- Smoking
- Drug and alcohol abuse
- Gangs
- Jail/Prison
- Child abuse/molestation
- Malnourishment, and
- A decrease in physical, mental, and spiritual wellbeing

Simply put: A fatherless child has a higher risk for a negative outcome in life.

Let me be clear here: **I do not think the father is the sole blame for those unfortunate issues.** However, his absence from the home or the life of his child has an enormous impact on that ugly reality. While there are many similarities in a child's life when the father is absent, girls tend to be more withdrawn, and boys tend to act out more. If the child is very young, they may not notice the absence of their father because they have no distinct memory of him being around—as opposed to an older child with many memories who may experience a total breakdown.

On the flip side, the presence of the father or father figure in the home could make the life of a child worse. How, you ask?

- ➢ If the father is present and abusive to the child or mother, he is **not** positively contributing to the child's life.
- ➢ If the father shows very little affection, he is **not** positively contributing to the child's life.
- ➢ If the father's role is "just a financial provider," he is **not** positively contributing to the child's life.
- ➢ If the father is selfish, choosing only to deal with his personal problems, he is **not** positively contributing to the child's life.

As you can see, in each instance, the father's presence can prevent the establishment of a nurturing family environment.

I do not and will not place all the blame on the father because there are many homes where the mother has left children behind with the father. Some of the reasons for leaving are not much different than when the father leaves the home:

- ➢ Irreconcilable differences
- ➢ The pursuit of another relationship
- ➢ A sense of personal inadequacy
- ➢ Alcohol and/or drug addiction

Some of the more surprising reasons come directly from women themselves. I have read more than 250 online posts of stories written by women who made the difficult decision to leave their children behind. I am not referring to those who have decided to pursue a better career or women in the military who left for an extended deployment. I am talking about women who are dealing with some emotional issues. I believe it is a mother's nature to be a protector of children, so when she decides to leave, it is generally due to unusual circumstances.

Most of the reasons provided in the online posts were attributed to the mother wanting to have a safer and more stable environment for their children, and they thought the father could provide those needs. That reasoning was followed by mothers who were dealing with their own emotional, medical, psychological, past trauma, and financial issues. They are difficulties that often go undetected and unresolved, thereby impacting the overall care of the children and highlighting why more attention should be given to those issues.

I was also encouraged to view online posts from some of the older children who experienced one of their parents leaving the home. I was pleased to find that many have forgiven the "absent parent." A few have reconciled the relationship with their parent, while others have decided to move on with their lives without that parent. There were also those who are still dealing with the emotional hole, anger, and depression they were left with from the absence of one or both parents. The emotional scars can last a lifetime and can impact their relationships as adults if not openly discussed with trusted loved ones or professionals. These children must not be forgotten.

In addition, I worry that as a society, we may not be totally conscious of how we view and label parents in those situations as a whole. We seem to accept, judge, and rationalize why fathers leave children behind while vilifying and labeling mothers as "abandoning their children." Either way, the children, mothers, and fathers all suffer.

The parents must take a hard look at their situation before deciding to leave. I do, however, understand there are some family dynamics and conditions that should be walked away from, but that does not excuse the fleeing parent from their responsibilities of caring for the children. Realizing that some situations can be a bit challenging at first, I believe if you stick with it and keep your focus on the children, the tables will soon turn for the better. For me, taking care of my responsibilities was and still is a part of my core being, so thinking otherwise or giving up was not an option.

When I first separated from my daughter, she was about five years old—a bright-eyed, pigtailed "Mini-Me" (without the mustache, of course). Regardless of the circumstances, I always took time for her, cherished our alone time, and ensured she knew I loved her. I did not need a court order to tell me when to visit or provide financial support and guidance for her. The walks, talks, games, piggy-back rides, and overall bonding that occurred during my daughter's early years are priceless. Even to this day, we have a strong bond and continue to build on our relationship.

I have also had the privilege of being a stepfather—or, as I like to say, a "step-up-father." When circumstances separated me from my stepdaughter, she was around 12 years old. Growing up, she was full of energy, the life of her little tea party, and a leader in her own right. On the daily ride home from the local afterschool program, I remember looking in the rearview mirror and seeing a talkative young lady who was always curious about her surroundings. I would often ask questions, just to see what was on her mind. I was never disappointed by her responses. I never knew what to expect because the replies were often gibberish, comical, on point, insightful, and often ahead of her time. During those moments, I knew the possibilities were limitless and that she would go as far as her vivid imagination would take her.

Leaving a significant other is usually a tough decision. Most often, you have invested a lot of time, resources, and energy to make the relationship work, but somewhere along the way, things took a turn for the worse, and life-changing events are put in motion. In the heat of the moment, the wheels can come off the serene family environment rather quickly, leaving a row of bodies in the rearview mirror. Unfortunately, the identification of the smaller bodies belongs to innocent children who had nothing to do with the decisions made by their parents. If you find yourself in this predicament, ensure you have built a strong, loving relationship early in your child's life. Equally important is ensuring you sustain the parent/child relationship, regardless of the circumstances, as it will help create an unbreakable bond through the years to come.

Over the years, being a single father has taught me this one important lesson:

Parenting is a full-time job, 24 hours a day, seven days a week.

As a parent, there are no days off, calling in sick, or getting someone else to work your shift. You are both owner and a floor worker. Therefore, the head must balance what goes on in the daily activities of the employees (in this case, the children) against the requirements of their high-yielding future. That is no easy task, but the overall success of the family depends on being in the now, having a plan, and keeping your eye on the external factors, all while maintaining a laser focus on the family's goals.

Just as a competent Chief Operating Officer (CEO) does, a good father manages the short-term, plans for the mid-term, and invests in the long-term. The CEO/father also sets values and standards that create an indelible and solid foundation to ensure the family's overall success.

PARENTING MEMOIR

Humble Beginning

Although I was born in Lewes, Delaware, I moved down south to stay with my grandparents as a small child. Youthful memories of riding my bicycle through the dark streets and roads of the small south Georgia town of Quitman played a big part in my humble beginning. Reaching top speed in a matter of a few seconds, I could have easily left any New York City bicycle courier in the dust! However, in our small town, there was no such thing as a bicycle courier. There were no protected bikeways or bike lanes, but only miles and miles of open paved and unpaved roads for my riding enjoyment.

At the center of town was the main courthouse building, which was one of my most important mile markers on my route to and from most of my destinations. It was important because I used the courthouse building as cover during the late hours of the night to shield myself from any crazies or local police that might be out on the street (I was blessed enough to not have any run-ins with either and was determined to keep it that way by keeping a low profile and being a responsible rider).

Often, I would hide behind the building to avoid being seen by drivers passing by late at night. As soon as the coast was clear, I would make a mad dash for the next milestone on my route: The 23-foot high South Court Street Bridge that was built in 1938. It was all downhill riding from the courthouse to the bridge, with no traffic lights to stop me along the way. As a kid, the length and height of the bridge made for a frightening experience when it came to walking or riding a bike across. By the time I made it to the bridge, my heart was always racing from maintaining the top downhill speed. Once I made it to the bridge, the road surface switched from asphalt to hard dirt.

From there, it was another two-mile hike down West Crawford Street, which ran adjacent to the CSX Transportation railroad tracks. There were houses along the way—some brightly lit by their porch light, illuminating what appeared to be unauthorized activities in the front yards. There were also several stretches of the street that were pitch black, making it almost impossible to see three feet in front of me. All I could hear were crickets and a few bullfrogs every now and then. Either way, I was okay with the fluctuating light and darkness because I figured I could outrun almost anything on my bicycle, to include any animal or car. Plus, I thought as many teenagers do: I was invincible! I was not worried once I approached my final turn toward home. From the railroad tracks (which I completely jumped most of the time), it was another dark but short stretch to my grandparents' house. I usually touched down in the yard right before curfew.

During the '70s, it wasn't a real necessity to lock the doors of your house. Most often, the back door to my grandparents' home was left open for me to enter without having to knock. However, as I got older (around 17 years old), I started staying out a little later than allowed. Several times, I pushed it a little over the limit but never crossed the line too far, mostly out of respect for my grandparents. If the back door happened to be locked, I would tap on my aunt's window. She would always get up and unlock the door—no questions asked (something I am still grateful for to this day). As I reflect on those times, I realize I was truly blessed that nothing happened while I was out late at night.

Remember: This was in the late '70s…in a small town in the deep south…that had a population of roughly 5,100 people, which was made up of 60% African American, 32% White, and the 'Other' category was comprised of Native Americans, Asians, and Hispanics. At the time, the 32% White ran everything in town and made no effort to hide it. (Although it was near the end of the '70s, it felt more like the '60s never quite turned the corner into the '70s.) I had a keen sense of awareness of the things that were happening in the South at the time, so I knew to keep my head down or look straight ahead when I went from 'point A' to 'point B.' We were not outright told where we could or could not go. Still, everyone on all sides knew to spend their time in their own neighborhoods or one that looked more like their own. As a matter of fact, even though we had White students since our schools fully integrated during the 1970-1971 school year (I was in the third grade at the time), when the bell rang at the end of the day, things were segregated again until the next school day. Most noticeably, there were no interactions with White students during Summer breaks whatsoever.

Today, times are a bit different. Most neighborhoods in the U.S. are integrated with people from all races and walks of life.

My children found some of my pre-integration school stories unthinkable. I shared those stories because not only did they need to know some of the things I experienced as a young man, they also needed to know and understand that the history of this country is not all good. They must be able to discern not all our history is as great as written in the school's history books. I also use a combination of my past with my present experiences as teaching moments to help them understand that regardless of where they come from, they can still learn from negative experiences and use them to their advantage.

TERRACE V. WHITE

The Root Cause

There are numerous reasons—far too many to name here—why a child may end up in a single-parent home or staying with a relative/close friend of the family. Whatever the reason, it could be either a good thing or have a devastating effect on the child for many years to come, especially if the parent neglects their responsibilities. The situation may not be as dramatic as the opening scene described previously, but children often blame themselves when one of the parents leaves or is consistently not around…especially the father.

The child may feel angry, isolated, and unwanted, or may not know what to feel. Even if there are other siblings in the home, a child could feel lonely. When one parent is present and accounted for and doing all those 'Superman' or 'Superwoman' things they do daily, the child always knows that something is not quite right. They may not talk about it or know how to express their feelings, but believe me, **they know.**

Being a father is much more than being a disciplinarian or primary breadwinner. Additional duties include being **physically**, **emotionally**, and **spiritually** present in the child's life. It also involves being **active** in their daily activities, regardless of how you feel about them, and how crazy their ideas may seem at the time. Think about how actors and actresses make themselves look like fools in some of the roles they play, all for the sake of a laugh. Well, my friend, making your children laugh uncontrollably is just one of many leading roles of a good father. *NO ONE* in the room should be funnier than you.

Just like actors and actresses, the fans do not see the hard work and behind-the-scenes preparation required to put on an award-winning show. Likewise, your children probably have no clue that you got up in the wee hours of the morning, ensured things were in order before leaving for work, spent hours in traffic, dealt with rude customers, and spent a considerable amount of time during the day wondering how the monthly bills were going to get paid. When they see you walk through the door at the end of the day, they see their **HERO** and the funniest, most important person that ever lived: their father.

If you asked fathers of today about their presence in their child's life, many would likely tell you they spend much more time with their child than their father did with them. My hope is this upward trend of real involvement will continue and that the old ways of thinking decrease or, better yet, be wiped off the face of the planet.

Being a stay-at-home father or not having a job simply because you do not want to work does not equate to being a responsible father just because you are physically in the home. I get that today, there are those families where the father stays at home, takes care of the children, does most of the housework, and sometimes runs a home business. However, most of the time, that type of arrangement is based on a mutual understanding and agreement between both parents. With the price of childcare these days, a stay-at-home father may be the best route to take for your family's requirements. If it works for all parties involved, go for it! I tip my hat to you! However, I implore you to be aware of the irreconcilable issues that may rear their ugly head when the dynamics of the family change, decisions are one-sided, there are misunderstandings, or there is no mutual agreement about who is responsible for what.

Since most of my child-rearing days were spent as a single father, it was easy for me to make decisions that were best for the family because there was no other voice than that of God to be taken into consideration. Of course, as my children got older, I included their voices (in most cases) before making a final decision. Depending on the situation, there were times when my voice was the loudest from start to finish. Also, I tried to be conscious of my overall tone, their facial expressions, and their body language because I learned over the years that if there is a breakdown in communication, my message would not be understood or received in a positive or constructive manner. Being mindful of that potential pitfall is imperative, especially when the other parent may not be around.

Family History

Have you ever wondered why you are the way you are or why you act the way you do? A lot of children grow up thinking about and asking their parents those exact questions. If you have not figured it out by now, those questions can go unanswered throughout your lifetime. Some people are never able to connect the dots or just never thought to ask about their family's history.

If that is your situation, allow me a moment to provide some assistance based on my experience.

For starters, I believe that God created us in His own image—not in the physical sense, but attributes such as character, emotions, and intellect. We are also perfectly made and were **not** created *"by accident."* We are not *"mistakes"* that are roaming the earth without a purpose. We were all created on this earth with the purpose of glorifying and honoring God. If you believe and can embrace that truth, you are well on your way to beginning the conversation with your children concerning your family's history.

PARENTING MEMOIR

Be open to answering any of the questions you are likely to be asked, even if you find yourself caught off-guard by your child's straightforward but innocent questions. Old-school parenting styles may lead you to think that your family's history should not be discussed at all.

When I was growing up, there were questions children just *knew* not to ask our parents or grandparents. What went on in the house stayed in the house, and the keys to family secrets were thrown away or only known by a few. Often, that was because the family's history included the elephant in the room that no one dared to or wanted to discuss. Every now and then, bits and pieces of the story would find their way to our little ears, but we never got the **missing** piece that would complete the puzzle.

If we were suspected of being too nosy or a snitch, that would be the end of our playtime for days on end. Our friends had only **one** opportunity to knock on the door to ask if we could come outside to play. After one stern *"NO!"* from the adult, they quickly got the message and went on to create memories without us because, after all, that stern warning did not apply to them. **We *knew* it was directed at us!**

Looking back, those seemed like hard lessons, but that is how life was during the '60s and '70s.

Over the years, I have made it a point and priority to share my family's history with my children. How did I learn the history, you ask? Well, it was quite simple: **I asked questions!** I sat at the feet of some of the older family members and was not afraid to ask the tough questions. Their childhood memories, challenges they faced while growing up in the south, daily interactions with their siblings, and, of course, the family recipes were all up for grabs. During those informational sessions, I was like a curious toddler on a sugar rush. I soaked in all the stories and information I could get.

I found out that on one side of the family, everything was lost in the 1930s during a hurricane that hit Florida. On the other side of the family, everything was lost in a house fire in Delaware. Although a lot of family history was lost during both events (i.e., pictures, documents, and irreplaceable mementos), those tragedies always pulled the family closer together.

As well, during those sessions, it was confirmed that a strong sense of family has always been important—not only in our immediate family but also in all past communities in which we lived. Families and neighbors looked out for each other in all areas of life. A person's possessions — including money, food, clothing, crops, and their precious time — were gladly shared with anyone in need. That sense of belonging and community is quite different today. Now, we barely know our neighbors or the needs of some of our own family members.

Another reason why I wanted to know more about my family's history was that I wanted to share the family's medical and health history with my children. Knowing that piece of our history gave me insight and a better understanding of similar aches and pains going on in our lives. In addition, those golden nuggets of information helped to develop a plan to reduce the risks or prevent related medical issues. For example, diabetes and hypertension have been unwelcomed staples on both sides of our family for years. Those health conditions can cause other risk factors such as heart failure, strokes, kidney failure, and even loss of limbs. The more you know about your family's health history, the quicker you can develop a game plan to put an end to those preventable conditions. Simple lifestyle changes such as increasing physical exercise, drinking more water, maintaining a healthy diet, and having a healthy spiritual and social lifestyle can make a world of difference!

It is also important to know and share your family's history with your children because of today's social media environment. Although it is a massive platform with millions of people using it for sharing information, ideas, and networking, it may not be as large as you think. What I mean here is that often, it is used as a place to connect with others for several reasons. There is always the possibility of connecting with a person and hitting it off, only to find out that person is actually a distant family member. Finding a family member on social media can be a blessing-turned-curse if not known in time, and the friendship "develops" into something more. That may be an awkward conversation to have, but it should be one you consider having with your children. **KNOW** your family's history!

After you have picked the minds of your immediate family members, consider browsing the numerous available websites to help with your research. Most of them provide the option to simply plug in a few details about your family member, such as the name, birthdate, date of death, and location for starters. I must warn you: A lot of the old records and documents available may have a few errors or be slightly "off" regarding the exactness of the details. Those mismatches may leave you wondering if the member you found is truly your deceased relative or not.

For example, during my family history search, I found several misspelled first names on the 1940's census records. Although the entries were handwritten during that time, there is no doubt which spelling is correct because those relatives are still alive today, and I know exactly who they are. Besides, the ages listed in some of the records reflect their age at the time the census was recorded, which proved to be helpful.

There are also other bits of information you may find that just might surprise you, such as family members' occupations and highest education levels.

Other areas I recommend you be made aware of are the exact birth and death dates of family members. Some dates may be one day off or one to two years off. I was able to verify the correct dates by talking to family members, viewing copies of obituaries I had saved from funeral services, and from researching cemetery records. A lot of the cemetery records had a picture of the gravestone with the birth and death dates, along with middle names. Accurately documenting information about your family members is extremely important because not only are you sharing it with your children, you are substantiating what you found and correcting any misstated details that were documented many years ago when similar tools and methods we have today were not available. Be forewarned: You can easily spend *hours and hours* researching databases during each research session.

Although your loved ones may no longer be alive, I found that it is important, refreshing, and necessary to visit their gravesites periodically. For many years, I put off taking trips to visit some of my loved ones' graves. However, during my family history research, the desire to do so grew more and more as time passed. Since I was so close to my grandparents, their gravesites were first on the list. I must admit that it was one of the most satisfying trips and time well spent. I stood there, not saying much. With my eyes closed, I took several deep breaths. While I know their spirits are not in the grave, it was such a relief to have finally made the trip to show my respects to the two most important people in my life. The only thing I would change is that I wish I could have shared that moment with my children—first, to show them exactly where the gravesites are located and second, to ensure they learn how to pay respect to their ancestors.

Every day of our lives, we write and add new events to our family's history. Therefore, we must share those events while they are fresh in our minds, never forgetting those who came before us.

PARENTING MEMOIR

Fellowship

Growing up in southern Georgia, attending Sunday morning church service was the foundation of the start of our week. When it came to attending church, my grandparents did not play around. As a kid, we had no choice but to participate. It never crossed my mind to test the water…*and I am not talking about being baptized.* I am referring to the mere **thought** of not going to church. If I did, I better be on my death bed or have one foot already in the grave! It was always in my best interest to sit there, be quiet, and act like I was paying attention. To be honest, the best parts for me were the singing and communion.

The choir consisted of adult men and women. The children had their own little group, of which I was not a part. The adults wore thick burgundy robes that moved in unison as they rocked from side to side. They almost made me sweat just looking at them. There were a few choir members who had no business being a part of the group. Either they missed their intended calling, or they were just being disobedient.

Every now and then, someone in the congregation would fall out, but I was not allowed to ask any questions for fear of my grandmother's deadly backhand. If she thought I was talking, asleep, or not paying attention during service, she would pop me without missing a hand clap. I learned quickly to only move my eyes if I wanted to "wander off." Anything that was going on behind me had to wait until the service was over.

Communion was always taken on the first Sunday of each month. For years, I wondered about the taste of that purple juice. I was not sure if it was pure wine (not that I had ever tasted real wine at that point) or grape Kool-Aid. The protocol was for each person who participated in communion to pass their empty golden cup to the end of the row for collection. One day, I noticed my grandmother had left a little extra in her cup. I looked down the row once, and then twice as the devil told me, *"Take a swig!"* In my mind, I knew I should have kept the rotation going down to the end of the row. However, my curiosity got the best of me. My taste buds were raring to go as I licked my lips and puckered up. Before the cup reached my mouth, I felt the wind from my grandmother's deadly backhand graze my ear. Due to a slight move to the right and my quick reflexes, she missed…but only by a hair. That was enough for me to treat that cup like a hot potato and usher it down toward the end of the row!

As I got older and was able to drive, I did not mind going to church because pulling into the church parking lot while behind the wheel made me feel like an adult. (Yes, I know my joy was for the wrong reason.) Regardless if I stayed out late the night before or not—which was any time past 11:30 p.m.— I had to get up no later than 8:00 a.m. the next morning to prepare for church. Most Sunday services lasted way past 2:00 p.m., and by then, I was brain dead. I cannot fail to mention that lunch/dinner was usually provided, so that broke the daydreaming into 'Part 1' and 'Part 2.'

Looking back, those early Sunday mornings helped to shape me into the man and father I am today. I cannot think of a better foundation on which to build a family than those examples and lessons learned. They are etched into my heart and mind to this day. What seemed like a marathon service each week turned out to be a master class on discipline, family, and how to conduct oneself. I am so grateful for those weekly experiences and opportunities because not only did they pour God's Word into my life at an early age, but they also poured an unshakable foundation that still stands.

Eventually, I graduated from high school and then joined the military, and that foundation traveled with me across the miles. Like most young people when they get away from home for the first extended time, I seemingly forgot some of those valuable lessons learned while growing up. Although I had been taught and knew right from wrong, my newfound freedom overwhelmed me, which turned out to be more like bondage. Through it all, however, those early lessons kept finding their way back to me. They gave me comfort during uncertainty and the hard times I had created for myself—so much so that after years of frustration, living away from God, doing it my way, and bumping my head repeatedly, I was touched by the mighty hand of God.

I recall the day...

I walked down the church aisle all alone in March of 1994, stumbling like a toddler. With great confidence, I gave my life to Christ that day. Through God's grace and mercy, coupled with those initial seeds planted by my grandparents, God's plan for my life was put in motion. I thank God every day for that—and He is not through with molding me yet. As the days are long, I am still learning and still pressing forward.

As a single father with very few answers, I often go to the well to draw a cool drink of water, remembering those lessons learned and experiences that have occurred during the last 50 years of my life. At my secret place that is reserved only for me to get my daily word from God, I gain rest, courage, and direction. Over time, I have found myself standing at the same deep well, not only during times of unrest but in good times, too. It became my place of refuge with an unlimited supply of the Fruit of the Spirit: **Love, Joy, Peace, Longsuffering, Goodness, Faithfulness, Gentleness, and Self-control.** It is at the same well where I remember the faces of those choir members who sang off-key but made the joyful sound of angels. My life has come full circle, and I now understand their dedication and steadfastness.

As a single father, I have been given great tasks that I am well-equipped to handle—tasks that include training up my children in which way they should go, just like I was trained. Therefore, no tasks are too big to accomplish, including raising my children. The key is to know that when I am weak, then I am strong. I must recognize where to go to harvest my Fruit of the Spirit.

In my home, I have several wells (secret places) that provide daily bread. One is the closet. On the surface, it may not seem like the ideal place to get nourishment and to gain knowledge, but on the inside, it provides a place that is insulated from outside noises and distractions. It allows me to pour my heart out to God—moments that are often filled with wandering phrases that only He can understand. Nonetheless, I just keep talking to Him without hesitation because I can feel there is no judgment and no hesitation to give me rest.

Another well in my house is the vacant room above the garage. That room was somewhat of a transition room because it was once occupied by my daughter during her last years of college and then by my son as he discovered his pathway in life. During that time, I called it "A Room to Go." Now, it is a place where I go to pray and read the Bible. I now call it "The Upper Room" because it is where I go to have my spirit-man fed and to receive instructions from God. Plus, I get a warm feeling from being physically closer to God. That may sound a bit crazy to some, but I encourage you to do whatever it takes to get you into that space and right frame of mind to hear your God-given assignment clearly. That is how you know it is the correct action to take and the right place to be.

The Mission Statement

In the business world, a Mission Statement is used to communicate the purpose of the business. Once it is finalized, it gives the organization its identity and sense of direction. As the business evolves, changes in core values, changes in its leadership, or changes due to real-world events may prompt a moment to rethink what is essential to the overall health of the organization. As a result, the Mission Statement may (or may not) change.

The statement is typically short, simple, to the point, and spells out the overall goal. Sometimes, it is confused with a Vision Statement, but they are completely different. The Mission Statement tells why you exist, while the Vision Statement tells you what is to be pursued.

Now that you have the basics, consider establishing a Mission Statement for your family. This should be taken seriously, especially if you find yourself in a single-parent role or are physically separated from your children. Begin by asking yourself this one question:

What is the overall goal I have for my children?

Once you have narrowed it down and established the goal, share it with your children. Just like in a business, your children are shareholders in your family and have a general interest and a legal right in the outcome. After all, they are directly impacted by each parent's decisions. As they get older, consider involving them in the decision-making process and re-creation of the family's Mission Statement. While the parent has the final say, never lose sight of their wants, needs, and desires. Periodically making changes to your well-thought-out Mission Statement will help the communication lines and love grow between you and your children. If done with thoughtfulness, the overall family relationship will remain fresh and clean, and not boring and stale.

Following are a few simple examples of parent/child Mission Statements. Remember to keep them short and sweet. If you really want to personalize it, replace *"my child/children"* with your child's name or children's names.

1. "To love, protect, educate, and inspire my child/children."
2. "Tend to the overall personal wellness and growth of my child/children."
3. "To positively nurture, teach, and inspire my child/children in such a way that they will want to share their memories with others."

PARENTING MEMOIR

4. *"To be the example, a rock-solid provider, and the funniest father in the world to my child/children."*

The sample Mission Statements are only provided to get your creative juices flowing as you create your own for your family. The entire idea of establishing a Mission Statement may seem a bit corny. The initial ideas may not flow freely. However, if you stay with the general idea and remember why you are creating such a statement, the ideas will begin to flow over time. At first, write down everything that comes to mind, regardless of how ridiculous it may sound when you read it aloud. In the beginning, do not worry about the length of the statement. You can always go back and adjust it when you have the basics down on paper. In the end, remember to keep it short, sweet, to the point…and **rememberable**.

TERRACE V. WHITE

The Treasure of Fatherhood

Fatherhood should not be taken for granted or taken lightly. It is like a hidden treasure waiting to be discovered. Whether the hunt to find the treasure is carefully mapped out or if you just stumble upon it, once you find it, it will be one of your most prized possessions. In fatherhood, your treasure is your children because they are one-of-a-kind-jewels, unlike a treasure hunt game where the treasure is in the hunt.

In the amazing world of Biology, the father plays a significant part in the reproductive process, whether he knows it or not. In the process, the father has both the X- and Y-chromosomes, while the mother only has the X-chromosome. The Y-chromosome is the child's gender-determining chromosome. Therefore, based on proven science, you can see the first major contributing factor of the father in a child's life from the very beginning.

Once the child arrives, the bonding begins. Besides the parental bond a father should establish with his child, he also has legal and social rights and obligations in the overall development of the child. The father should strive to be present in every aspect of his child's life by taking personal responsibility for choices that impact the family. Being present is much more than being physically present, though. It includes financial support, spiritual guidance, teaching life skills, educational direction, and providing unconditional love…to name a few. A good father should also have and display basic traits and characteristics such as having a love for God, patience, self-control, leadership qualities, and be a nurturer worthy of respect.

If you never knew your biological father, never spent much time with him, or never really had a father figure, it could subconsciously have a lasting impact on you. It can affect the way you feel about yourself and the way you treat others, including your own children. Some men feel like they are too inadequate to be a good father. If you find yourself becoming overwhelmed by the magnitude of your obligations or have a lack of desire to follow through, remember this: **YOU ARE NOT ALONE.** There is no better example of what a good father is and looks like than the Father of Heaven and Earth, the Creator of All Things, the Great I Am, and the King of Kings — the Almighty God.

Our sufficiency comes from God. When He looked at everything He had made, He was pleased. Therefore, from the very beginning of time, you were made perfect in His own image. In those moments of doubt (they will come), you must remember that truth not only for yourself but also for you to embrace so that you can share it with your children. They, too, need to know how to combat doubt when it creeps into their mind. God loves us and will give up whole nations to draw us to Him because we are precious in His sight. Therefore, stand on the promises of God, especially in those times of doubt.

Following are a few passages of scripture from the New International Version (NIV) of the Holy Bible that helped me get through a few tough times:

- *"Be strong and of good courage, do not fear nor be afraid of them; for the Lord your God, He is the One who goes with you. He will not leave you nor forsake you"* **(Deuteronomy 31:6)**.
- *"Fear not, I am with you; be not dismayed, for I am your God. I will strengthen you; I will uphold you with My righteous right hand"* **(Isaiah 41:10)**.
- *"Trust in the Lord with all your heart, and lean not on your own understanding; in all your ways, acknowledge Him, and He shall direct your paths"* **(Proverbs 3:5-6)**.
- *"Be anxious for nothing, but in everything by prayer and supplication, with thanksgiving, let your requests be made known to God. And the peace of God, which surpasses all*

understanding, will guard your hearts and minds through Christ Jesus" **(Philippians 4:6-7).**

➢ *"I can do all things through Christ who strengthens me"* **(Philippians 4:13).**

➢ *"For God has not given us a spirit of fear, but of power and of love and of a sound mind"* **(2 Timothy 1:7).**

Fear is an unpleasant emotion that causes you to be afraid. You may feel threatened, terrified, experience pain, or suddenly be startled by some outside source. You may not even recognize that you are fearful of something until it is brought to your attention.

Have you ever asked yourself, *"From where does fear come?"* Surely, it did not come from God. It is likely it originated in your mind because of the unknown about a situation. Think about it like this: From the very beginning and without putting any thought into any given situation, you have a 50% chance of success and a 50% chance of failure. You can either like or dislike something. You can go up or down. Either way, no matter the situation, you will always have those 50/50 odds, even before you burn up one brain cell trying to figure things out.

So, when fear comes knocking on your door (and it will), let your faith answer. Fear cannot enter or do anything to you without your permission and cooperation. Do not invite it in.

There are numerous types of fears and phobias, to include:

- The fear of failure
- The fear of being judged
- The fear of being rejected
- The fear of spiders/bugs/creeping things
- The fear of losing everything you have worked for
- The fear of not being good enough
- The fear of public speaking
- The fear of heights
- The fear of being successful
- From my time spent as a single father, I would argue that single-parenting could be added to the list of fears.

In general, being a parent is as real as it gets — especially single-parenting…since there is so much to learn. The fear of having to care for a precious little soul that you helped bring into this world may bring some anxiety, but do not be alarmed. Those initial feelings are pretty normal.

For me, the trials of fatherhood have produced a whirlwind of emotions over the years. There were many twists, turns, ups, and downs. However, I always remembered that fear was not a part of my destiny. Therefore, I recognize it, accept it for what it is, assign meaning, and then quickly dismiss it.

For years, I have heard people say that hairdressers wear the worst hairstyles; carpenters have the worst houses; mechanics own the worst cars; financial advisors need financial advisement themselves; instructors make the worst students; and a lot of therapists need therapy. While I do not mean to bash anyone here, I have noticed that depending on your outlook, in some cases, those observations are not far from the truth. Still… **Who is to say what is worst and what is better?**

Quickly dismissing those widely held ideas, I could not help but wonder if I was qualified to write a book on parenting. Using a similar thought process as the myths mentioned, does that mean parents who write parenting-related books or give parenting advice are "worst parents"? While there is no evidence that any of that is true, that ideology may provide insight and encourage you to explore any parenting challenges you may encounter.

Ask yourself the following (and answer honestly):

Am I giving parenting advice to others but not following my own advice?

Are my children lacking because I am too busy analyzing the household and parenting skills of others?

If you think about it, they are valid points that should be explored a bit further and, perhaps, applied to your own family dynamic. It is easy to give advice to others, but you must make sure you pay attention to your own.

I would like to think I have taught my children a lot about life in general. I have learned a tremendous amount from them, as well. They helped make me the man I am today. They have taught me how to be a better man, father, and provider. Most of all, I have learned how to love, be patient, and forgive. I wanted to be the "perfect" father. I told myself that making mistakes was not an option and that I must lead by example. Well, guess what? While that is extremely nice to say and is something to shoot for, you can throw it all out the window because no one is perfect—parents and children included.

Remember: You cannot do it alone. I believe that is the way God intended it to be. He wants us to depend on Him and

Him alone for all our needs, including handling those uncertain times when parenting.

In the world of Track and Field, the official starter of the race usually says, *"On your mark"* or *"Take your mark."* That directs the runners to get into position and prepare for the race ahead. If they choose to ignore the command and not get into the proper position, they can quickly get off track or, even worse, be disqualified.

In the sport of Bowling, there are markings and arrows in the center of each lane. The purpose of those markings is to help guide the ball to the center pin and improve the bowler's overall accuracy. If they aim left or right of the center marking, the ball will travel in that direction or even worse, into the gutter.

In the sport of Archery, the target includes a black center that is part of concentric circles. The idea is to hit the center or get as close to it as possible.

As a parent, you may not hit your mark all the time. You may be a bit slow off the starting block. However, with concentration, focus, help from others, and God's grace, you will hit your mark or get closer to your goal more times than not. The path for your family is already paved, with plenty of markers along the way. We get into trouble when we take a detour or the wrong exit.

Imagine traveling across the United States in a car for the first time. You have the option of taking main highways or one of the numerous rural roads. However, you stand the possibility of getting lost using those back roads, and the trip will take much longer to reach your destination. In the United States, when traveling from East to West, there is Interstate 10 on the southern route and Interstate 70 on the northern route. Traveling North to South, there is Interstate 95 on the east coast or Interstate 5 on the west coast.

As a parent, you may not know which route to take, but the main thing is to start the journey and adjust accordingly. Believe the things you need will be provided and that people will be strategically placed in your life to assist and listen to you while you are on your journey, and God will be your guiding light.

PARENTING MEMOIR

God Will Provide

Have you ever tossed and turned in the bed due to a sleepless night? You may have gone to bed at a decent hour, only to find yourself wide awake at 1:30 a.m., staring at a blinking light from the DVD player, watching the second hand on the clock going around and around, or trying to figure out every little noise you think you hear. What has only been a few minutes since the last time you checked the clock seems like hours.

I am sure we have all had those nights when, for some reason or another, we just cannot quiet our thoughts. As soon as we attempt to settle down a bit, an unwanted thought enters our mind and interrupts our peace and stillness. Too many of those nights in a row are abnormal and unhealthy. Soon enough, the days and nights appear to blend into one long and continuous nightmare.

If you have "been there, done that," you are not alone. Recently, I had one of those nights.

After a long day of completing chores around the house, walking on the treadmill, eating a hot meal, and taking a long, hot shower, I was primed for a good night's sleep. I laid down around 10:00 p.m. (my usual time to wind down), believing I would sleep through the night. However, my night did not quite go as planned. It was repeatedly interrupted by short bursts of uncontrollable thoughts. I am sure I raised my head from the pillow no less than 20 times, squinting my eyes each time at the clock to be sure time was not standing still. At first, I was not sure if it read 12:30 a.m. or 2:30 a.m., although I hoped for the latter because that would have meant I had gotten enough sleep to get me through the day. Well, that was wishful thinking! Once the fog cleared, I saw that the clock clearly read 12:30 a.m.

My mind began to race as I tried to determine if there was anything negative on my mind that kept me from resting peacefully. I wanted so badly to organize my thoughts. That relentless yearning only proved to double the pace and increased the number of thoughts running through my mind, which did not help at all. As a matter of fact, it made it worse!

I got up out of bed to a cold house and immediately went to the refrigerator. Standing in the kitchen with the refrigerator door open only made me colder. There were all types of leftovers and goodies staring me smack in the face, calling my name. After about five solid minutes of indecisiveness, I realized that selecting anything from the refrigerator at that time of the morning was not a good idea for my stomach, especially since I had plans to go back to sleep. I finally settled on bottled water to blanket the temptation and quench my thirst.

Like a toddler taking their first steps, I managed to stumble back to bed. Although part of my mind was in a much better place, it was not completely settled.

What was it that had me so restless?!

It was then I remembered that the only thing that truly quieted my mind was talking to God. The mental light came on immediately. I thought to myself, *"You big dummy! That option was there all along because God is always there and will never leave you!"* Remembering the source of my joy, I picked up my Bible. The restlessness subsided, and a big, uncontrollable smile set in on my face. I knew it would not be long before I heard a word from God, and my sleepless night would be bound and cast into Never-Never Land. Not only did I believe I would hear a word from God, but I also believed I would hear the right word in my time of need.

Still unsure of what I needed or, more importantly, what God wanted to tell me, I opened my Bible and began to pray for guidance. Surely enough, I landed on the passage of scripture that seemed to be written specifically for me: Genesis 22. For those of you unfamiliar with that chapter of the Bible, it is the account of when God tested Abraham by telling him to take his son, Isaac, and sacrifice him as a burnt offering. That must have been a tough pill to swallow!

Just imagine: You are told to take your own son and sacrifice him as a burnt offering. Back in those days, a burnt offering was the primary form of sacrifice and was a gift to God, showing their appreciation for His goodness or atonement of sin. As wild as the request seemed, Abraham was obedient and did exactly as God instructed. He even made Isaac carry the wood, flint, and knife that were to be used during the sacrifice. (That is worse than being told to get a wide belt or a switch made of fresh, slender green trigs, just so you could get a spanking with it!) On many levels, there was something just not right about God's request. Nonetheless, Abraham remained obedient.

As I read about halfway through Genesis 22, it hit me as to why that chapter was chosen for that time and place. It also explained what it was that kept me awake at night. I quickly remembered that for the past three to four months, I wrestled with a few things in my mind — things I had told myself I had to let go, yet subconsciously, I still held on while trying to control the outcome. Most of those things were centered on decisions my son was about to make for his future.

As parents, it is easy for us to see pitfalls, potholes, and see ahead around those sharp curves on the road of life. Most have traversed many, many rocky roads, giving us the advantage of knowing where the hazards are located, why we missed exits, and where we were when we completely ran off the side of the road and crashed. In my humble opinion, it is parental instinct to try to prevent your children from getting into obvious accidents or want to take the steering wheel away from our children completely. **Theoretically**, that is not a bad thing. Most often, however, that will not work for our children or us.

Moreover, we want to turn our children into "Mini-Mes," meaning we want them to follow the exact same or similar paths that we followed. After all, it is a formula that has been tested and proven to be successful…or at least it worked for us.

So, the picture became even clearer as to why that chapter of the Bible was chosen and how it related to the things that were on my mind. You see, I already had a similar episode of sleepless nights about three months earlier. After a few nights of tossing and turning, I prayed and talked to God about the things on my mind at that time. Ironically, that awakening also occurred at 12:30 a.m. For that situation, God told me exactly what to do to take care of the issues and move on with life. I was obedient—just like Abraham was with his son, Isaac, but on a much smaller scale, of course.

Now that I think about it, whether the issues are small or large, obedience is obedience. Any other action means disobedience.

After Abraham's obedience, he named that place on the mountain **"God Will Provide."** Therefore, for all the parenting issues I face, I try to stand on God's Word, be obedient, move on, and leave the consequences to Him. Once I remembered that truth, a big sigh of relief came over me. I could not wait to turn out the lights and go back to sleep. That night, I slept for about eight hours, woke up refreshed, and had a settled mind. Over time, I made reading God's Word a regular part of my day and is the first option I turn to when my head needs to be cleared of crazy thoughts.

I also found reading my Bible soothing when dealing with unexplainable body aches and pains. For example, for roughly five months, I experienced nerve issues in my right upper arm, neck, and shoulder area. The pain was excruciating and almost unbearable at times. I carefully thought about my activities over the prior month or so, yet I could not pinpoint anything I had done out of the ordinary that could cause such pain. It had completely shut down my normal daily activities, to the point I could not lift my right arm at all. Plus, there was tremendous pressure in the middle and on the right side of my chest that extended through my right armpit, tricep, bicep, and down to the elbow. It felt like a 50-pound weight was tied to my arm, pulling on the entire right side of my body. The slightest movements such as turning over in the bed at night, turning the doorknob, coughing, and sneezing intensified the pain even more. There were a few times when I almost dropped to my knees from the pain. It was a stabbing, aching pain, unlike anything I had ever experienced before.

I ended up going to the emergency room two times within a two-week period, along with a visit to my Primary Care Doctor. They ran all kinds of tests, including bloodwork, two EKGs, X-rays, and even an MRI. The tests showed **nothing** out of the ordinary. It was a puzzling and extraordinary time for the doctors because I was in so much pain with no definitive answers to the reason why. At one point, I thought the doctors began to think I was making things up, but that was far from the truth.

After weeks of being in pain and dealing with the uncertainty, I had an *"A-HA! Moment."* I remembered to stand on the Word of God, just as I had done numerous times before. I needed to not lean on my own understanding (or the doctor's). I had always known about the revelation but must admit that at the time, I had not put it into practice often enough.

I began to read all the scriptures I could find concerning healing. I meditated on passages such as Isaiah 41:10, Isaiah 53:5, and Luke 7:21. Each gave me great comfort during my physical pain and suffering. I also took the focus off myself and started meditating on God and His promises. The time I spent laying in the bed in pain led to a more deep-seated desire to spend time with God and understand Him, which eventually led to a full recovery with no explanations from the doctor — and a clearer understanding of the purpose of my life.

Could that have been God's plan all along? I believe that it was. Much to my disappointment (in myself), it got to a point where I had to be completely still and physically suffer for a while before God gained my full attention. From that point forward, my quiet time with God increased, and I began to see and live my purpose.

Unfortunately (some might say 'fortunately'), those types of episodes of being physically constrained are all too familiar. While we do not know precisely when it will happen, I think we can all agree that at some point in life, everyone will recognize those times when we live life in the fast lane and are doing "it" all by ourselves, only to be stopped in our tracks by a physical ailment.

As parents, those types of events in our lives must be shared with our children at the right time. Why? Because those times will come in your children's lives as well. The more you share your experiences, the more aware they will be of the pitfalls of living in the fast lane and trying to do "it" alone.

There is good news, though! God will always provide everything you need when you quiet your mind and listen for and to His voice!

Medicine, Exercise, and Healthy Eating

When it comes to healthy eating, my story is quite unique from any others you may have read or heard. You see, I am an average-sized African American male in my late 50s (at the time of this writing) with an athletic build. I have never had a problem with my weight, cholesterol, heart disease, strokes, cancer, nor any other major health issues. I have always had a high metabolism and can eat whatever I wanted whenever I wanted. I have always been strong, quick on my feet, and mentally and physically able to try and play any sport.

Although I have those attributes, I have always had a keen sensitivity about my weight. In my mind, based on my peers and sporting activities, I thought I should be at least 10 to 15 pounds heavier. Growing up, I was often teased about being on the "smaller" size. However, those falsehoods that were cast upon me made me strive to be the best I could be at everything, including sports.

How many of you know that being physically bigger is not always better? To conquer big things, you must start with the right mentality. Having the right mindset can put you well in front of your competition.

How many of you know that because you may not have a weight problem and may be of average size, you still may not be healthy? Based on what we put in our bodies, plaque can build up in the arteries and eventually harden. That controllable process does not discriminate and does not care if you are of small or large stature. It will attack any living, breathing body.

I grew up eating foods grown right in my grandfather's garden (or they were abundantly and readily available within a rock's throw from our neighbors). We had all types of greens and beans, tomatoes, squash, cucumbers, watermelons, cantaloupes, sweet potatoes, figs, apples, pears, blueberries, strawberries, kumquats, sugar cane, pecans, and peanuts…just to name a few. By today's definition, I guess you can say we were eating organic foods back in the '60s and '70s because I never saw my grandfather use any type of pesticides or fertilizers in the garden. He only used a compost matter to condition the soil—some having a strong "earthy" smell, so you can imagine what the mixture contained. Of course, he always finished the garden off with water, sunshine, and lots of tender loving care. The soil was dark, full of nutrients, and naturally perfect for growing plants. Unwanted invaders like weeds and grasses were immediately attacked by hand and replaced with lots of love.

With all that goodness right at our fingertips, the bad was also present. We balanced the healthy foods picked fresh from the garden with the typical soul foods like all types of cakes and macaroni and cheese made with thick, government-provided cheese. Those dishes were usually washed down with powdered government milk, extra-sweet tea that only a southerner can make, or a cold mason jar filled with our favorite original flavored Kool-Aids known as "Goofy Grape," "Raspberry," or plain "Orange." And who can forget the Kool-Aid mascot—the Kool-Aid Man with the catchphrase, *"OH, YEAH!"* Looking back, that phrase should have been, **"OH, NOOO!"** because most families filled one container with enough sugar to make **three** containers of Kool-Aid!

Our breakfast often included thick-sliced bacon, grits, and fresh biscuits made from scratch, topped with homemade preservatives. Our weekly dinner meals also included every part of the chicken you can think of, from the beak to the feet. Unless it was smothered in country gravy, it was usually cooked in thick white lard or reused grease sitting in a covered tin can on the back of the stove. In the end, it was all "died, fried, and laid to the side." Although the meals were made with love and were quite tasty, the heavy feeling they left behind made us suffer.

As I have gotten older, I have noticed an increase in aches and pains with varying degrees. In my mind, this new norm was tied to the regular symptoms of the aging process. For the first time in my life, I was put on a low-dosage blood pressure medication. To make myself feel better, I rationalized and decided the cause was due to job-related stress. That rationalization was partly true because I did have an incredibly stressful job at the time. However, I knew I had to face reality and determine the real reason I felt that way.

I looked closer at my overall lifestyle and made a few immediate changes I thought would help my health issues, especially since my daily activities started to be impacted. The changes were nothing too major. I just added a little more aerobic type exercises and yoga and decreased the amount of spicy foods I consumed. After making those minor changes, I noticed a little improvement.

I also noticed something else that made my eyebrows rise and confirmed I needed to consider making more significant changes.

In a man's mind, one thing that **always** gets our immediate attention is when our *"little buddy"* does not salute in the morning. Our *"little buddy"* has been with us from birth and through thick and thin, and when **he** decides he is not going to come out and play, **"HOUSTON, WE HAVE A PROBLEM!"**

When that happened to me, no one had to tell me twice that I needed to make more changes to improve my health. Immediately, I made an appointment to see my doctor.

While waiting to see the doctor, I had a highly informative conversation with the nurse about a wide range of medical topics, including blood pressure medications. When she asked me for the name of my current medication, and I told her, she shot me a surprised look. She went on to tell me that over the years, a lot of African American men had complained about the side effects of that exact same blood pressure medication and that I should talk to my doctor about it.

With that new information, I had a brief discussion with my doctor about my concerns with the performance of my *"little buddy."* In response, she changed my medication. Shortly after that change, I beefed up my exercise routine, and my blood pressure returned to within the normal range within a week or so. It must also be noted that my *"little buddy"* greeted me every morning, just as he did before.

At that point, I was feeling good, looking good, and mentally in an exceptionally good place. For some reason, I got the bright idea that I no longer needed to take the blood pressure medication and decided to stop…cold turkey. After three days with no issues whatsoever, the consequences of my decision hit me like a ton of bricks. Suddenly, I was gasping for air, and my heart was racing, feeling as if it were about to leap out of my chest. I then started sweating like someone poured a bucket of water on me. After I became disoriented and my vision blurred, all I can remember was riding in the ambulance and then counting the ceiling lights as they hurried me down the hospital's hallway. Thankfully, they were able to get my blood pressure down within a few hours.

The moral of my story is this: Once you are on blood pressure medication, you cannot just stop taking it. Specifically, you cannot go cold turkey.

As the years went by, I continued to monitor my blood pressure and improve my diet. Admittedly, I continued to eat what I wanted when I wanted. Soon, I began to notice more joint and muscle aches. They were not the ordinary aging-related squeaks and tweaks, either. They were more like the "I can barely move!" joint and muscle aches, causing me to miss several days of work because I was often awake half the night, tossing and turning during those flare-ups.

After mentioning those episodes to my friend, Dr. Bradley, she shared her discovery and motivation behind her *Kale Yeah, It's Good…No Meat Necessary* Vegan Cookbook. That book sat on my kitchen counter for about a month before I chose to pick it up and really start looking at the recipes. The pictures of the food drew me in, and the recipes appeared easy to follow.

My first thought: *"I am **not** trying to become a Vegan!"*

My second thought: *"I am **not** trying to lose weight!"* (Remember: I have been truly blessed with never having a weight problem.)

As the aches and pain flare-ups occurred more frequently, I then thought, *"What do I have to lose? I will try some of the recipes."* For me, it was not about my weight; it was more about adopting healthier eating habits and a wholesome lifestyle.

For starters, the food preparation time was right down my alley. It was quick and easy to top off the recipes and tasted much better than I thought. After a few weeks of eating healthily, I noticed the frequency and intensity of my aches and pains decreased drastically. In addition, I lost about ten pounds of unwanted waste that was not good for my overall gut health.

How many of you know that once you decide to make changes in your life for the better, something **always** tries to creep in to steal your joy?

As previously mentioned, I have always been a bit sensitive about my weight and thought that losing ten pounds was too much. Therefore, I got yet another bright idea to test my foolish theory that states:

"Food does not have anything or very little to do with my aches and pains."

I decided to revert to my old eating habits, which included eating what I want when I want. Well, it did not take long to determine my theory was wrong. As a matter of fact, my issues got **worse**! That time, I had developed a lot of nerve sensitivity throughout my body, mostly in my elbows, forearms, and hands. If you have never experienced nerve sensitivity or pain, know that it is a bit different than normal muscle and joint pains. I liken it to plucking the nerves with a guitar pick. It is a shooting pain that radiates up and down your limbs, making it virtually impossible to determine the exact origin of the pain. Sometimes, it is a stabbing sensation; other times, it is a chronic prickling, tingling, or burning feeling.

The moral of this part of my story is this: Food has **a lot** to do with aches, pains, and inflammation in the body.

After seeking expert advice from Dr. Bradley again, she recommended that I follow her previous instructions. She also shared her *The 21-Day Vegan Challenge* book with me. It is a resource for people who are interested in changing to a plant-based diet or even becoming a Vegan. I always thought plant-based and Vegan diets were one and the same. After further research, I learned there is a difference, mainly in the amount of fruits, vegetables, and animal products you consume.

While I am no expert and have just merged onto the road of changing to a plant-based diet, I am convinced the small changes I have already made have impacted my nerve-related issues for the better. Therefore, based on my experimentation and firsthand knowledge, I would encourage anyone with chronic issues to start taking a hard look at the foods being consumed, even if completely changing to a plant-based diet or becoming a Vegan is not appealing. The key is to make better food choices and act today!

I shared with you my personal story and perspective because I care. I care because too many people have suffered unnecessarily from preventable sicknesses and diseases. I care because it is up to you—as a parent—to ensure your children receive the proper nutrition as they grow. It is up to you to educate yourself and your children on how to choose healthier foods and ingredients. Knowing what I know now, I take advantage of the golden opportunity that has been presented to me by choosing to eat the right foods and healthy eating a family affair.

By no fault of their own, children will choose the sweetest or saltiest treats before opting to eat more fruits and vegetables. As daunting of a task as it may seem, I encourage you to take your children to the grocery store with you. Do your homework and then share with them how to choose fruits, vegetables, and healthier food choices. You can even make up a game and allow them to explore the various aisles to discover the foods that God created from the trees and plants for our consumption and enjoyment.

Up to this point, you may not have given too much thought about your eating habits, or you know you need to make changes and just have not done it. Do not be afraid to take that next step. Sometimes, you may think no one can relate to your eating and health challenges. You tell yourself that your story is unlike anyone else's. However, I have found that if you remain open and honest and start sharing pieces of your journey, you will learn your story is not much different than the next parent's account. Seek a way to weave a strong and healthy safety net for your children.

Lastly, while we are on the subject of health, let's briefly address the pandemic that has forever rocked over 180 countries and life in the United States as we've known it. The name of the disease is Coronavirus Disease 2019, abbreviated as COVID-19. In COVID-19, 'CO' stands for "Corona," 'VI' for "Virus," and 'D' for "Disease." Formerly, the disease was referred to as the 2019 Novel Coronavirus. It impacts a person's upper-respiratory-tract with symptoms that include mild to severe respiratory illness, accompanied by fever, cough, and difficulty breathing.

The disease has touched all walks of life, industries, and races. Like other deadly diseases such as diabetes, cancer, strokes, and high blood pressure, COVID-19 hit the African American community hard, and my family was not spared. At the time this book is being written, African Americans account for 30% of the reported cases of COVID-19 but are dying from the disease at a higher rate of their population share. Unfortunately, we have an incomplete picture of the toll the disease has on various communities. I am hopeful that soon, the states and the Center for Disease Control will capture and make that data available to the public.

When a disease comes along that has such devastating impacts on our daily lives, we must take it seriously. We must ensure we are educated about the disease and learn the preventive measures to take to avoid getting sick. Know the facts and be willing to share them with others, especially your children. There are so many conspiracy theories and theorists out there, causing the facts to get distorted quickly.

As parents, we must use our God-given intelligence, pay attention, and discern the truth. Remember always that your children want and need their parents around for a long time — and we want and need our children around. Therefore, keep the faith and do not let your guard down when it comes to infectious diseases and your overall health.

Full Circle

Every now and then, there are events that occur in your life that you just know will be life-changing. Such an event occurred during one of the Executive Leadership Development courses I attended for my job. The purpose of the course was to help develop professional and personal goals in order to make attendees better leaders. There were 24 students in the class, and each student was paired with a life coach to help them develop an action plan to achieve agreed-upon goals.

Before starting the class, each student completed a 360-Degree Feedback Survey. The purpose was to provide feedback on my current skills, as well as assist with developing new skills and behaviors. The results of the survey gave the coach an idea of my existing skill levels and how I operate in different environments and under changing conditions. A similar survey was also completed by my supervisors, superiors, peers, and subordinates in order to get a total 360-degree view of my skills and behaviors as seen through their eyes.

My coach's name was Michelle. Michelle was a very warm and highly recommended coach who had the credentials to back up the position she occupied. I was even more impressed with her overall approach to goal-setting. During our initial one-on-one coaching session, which was scheduled for three hours, things went in a slightly different direction than I originally anticipated. The conversation did not open with the textbook outline of determining my goals or developing the action plan to achieve those goals. Instead, to my surprise, it was more personal. I noticed she was not taking notes, with the focus specifically on the coach getting to know me on a deeper, personal level.

For starters, Michelle wanted to know about my background, upbringing, likes, and dislikes. Since I consider myself to be a very private person, I initially found her approach a bit overboard because I was not used to sharing such intimate details with a stranger. However, her personal approach put me at ease, and I quickly decided to trust the process, tell my truths, and be as transparent as possible.

Our open conversation continued and quickly turned to the subject of my upbringing. I shared things I had not thought about in years—things I had not shared with anyone else. In addition, I uncovered a few things I did not know about myself (or at least had not given them too much thought). One area that really struck a nerve was when Michelle asked me about my parents and grandparents. Since I was raised by my grandparents, we had a special bond. I always felt awfully close to them, especially my grandfather. She then asked me what type of people my grandparents were and how do I think they influenced my life and decision-making processes. She also asked, *"If your grandfather were sitting in the room with us today, what would he say about you?"* I never really tied the two together and always kept my personal and professional lives separate. However, after giving it some thought, I quickly realized that my upbringing had and has an enormous impact on my decision-making processes in both my personal and professional lives. That was truly another **"A-HA! Moment"** — one I will never forget. As I thought more and more about the question, I became overwhelmed and cried tears of joy as I thought about my grandfather sitting in the same room, providing his feedback during our coaching session. Out of nowhere, the tears began to flow uncontrollably because clear as a sunny day, I heard my grandfather say, *"I am so proud of you."*

Those words kept echoing in my mind. You see, my grandfather passed away in 1981, and my grandmother passed away in 1996. While I miss them both dearly, I especially miss my grandfather. He was a quiet man who handled his day-today business, took care of his family, and did not complain. After the release of tears that seemed to have been pinned up inside, I realized it all started there. My upbringing had a significant impact and helped to pave the way to my personal and professional decisions, as well as influenced my leadership style.

That feedback made me think that my parenting style is a combination of my grandmother and grandfather. My grandmother had a mild authoritarian parenting style. It was usually her way, no way, or the highway! There was mild punishment, a lot of respect, and often a one-way conversation—all sprinkled with her unconditional love. Conversely, my grandfather had more of an authoritative style. He enforced the rules and explained the consequences of breaking them, all while taking our feelings into consideration. Our conversations always flowed in two directions. Everyone showed him respect, including those in our community.

As I think about my grandfather and the times we shared, I realize he had a greater influence on my life than I previously thought, which laid the solid foundation of who I am today. The vivid memories I have of him after a long day in those hot, humid fields or our garden will never be forgotten. Every night after dinner, he would sit in his favorite chair to watch the evening news. His chair had wooden arms and legs like a side chair, with a slightly worn floral pattern and removable pillow for extra back support. During the evening news, he would often hold his head back and close his eyes. Perhaps he just wanted a moment to catch his breath, or he had drifted off to a faraway place. Much later, I found out that when his eyes were closed, he was simply praying. Back then, I am sure he had a lot on his mind and a lot to pray about. As children, we were unaware of his discomforts or hardships. I heard him when he prayed aloud for the family and our overall wellbeing. I never really had the chance to ask him what he silently prayed about, but I can imagine he prayed that his sugar cane and tobacco crops would reap maximum prices at the local market.

As a child, I did not pay too much attention to what went on in the day-to-day life of our family (or the world, for that matter). One thing I do know is that the images of my grandfather sitting in his favorite chair are forever etched in my mind. As a matter of fact, I have a favorite chair in my current home that is much like my grandfather's. It is a brown, medium-sized, soft leather recliner. My chair sits right beside my bed and a big window where I can look outside into the wooded area. It is usually my place of refuge after a hard day's work where I can watch the news, read an enjoyable book, or simply watch the squirrels, birds, and rabbits play. When it is raining, I often zone out by listening to the calming rain and watch as the wind waltzes with the trees. They would bend almost to the point of breaking but never have.

One day, I was sitting in my favorite chair reading the Bible when, out of nowhere, I started thinking about my grandfather. Scenes of him sitting in his chair, relaxing after a hard day's work, flooded my mind. I immediately began to pray and thought about how those two points in time—separated by 40 years—were playing out. From that day on to this very day, I sit in my chair to gain inspiration and motivation from the thoughts of my grandfather.

My peaceful thoughts were often interrupted by one of my children. However, I did not mind because 40 years earlier, I was that curious child who interrupted my grandfather's thoughts. Those moments of recollection made me smile. I would quickly close my eyes and hold my head back—just like my grandfather did—then thank God for the memories.

PARENTING MEMOIR

It's All About the Money

The more you know about any given subject, the more you can navigate the pitfalls and enjoy what it has to offer. Conversely, the **lack** of information or knowledge can prove detrimental and cost you more than you think. That is especially true as it relates to money management, which includes tracking expenses, budgeting, investing, banking, and taxes.

With today's technology, access to financial information is readily available at the touch of a few keystrokes. Almost every household has some type of access to the Internet through a cable provider or phone service. The problem comes when we do not take advantage of what is available—something that could be due to a lack of personal motivation, not having an interest in the subject, or not realizing how important it is to educate oneself on financial matters. Often, we put things off and wait until we are backed into a corner, forced to act. Things like technological advances are one driving factor that forces us to pay attention and grasp new ideas, especially when it touches our hard-earned money.

Financial literacy basically means possessing the skillset and knowledge that allows you to make good and effective financial decisions. If you do not already know how to manage your money, your children will force you to become more financially savvy just to survive. When you educate yourself and take advantage of the trove of available resources related to money management, you will be better prepared to tackle any financial difficulty that may arise.

Additionally, try thinking outside of the box by pushing yourself to devise new money solutions. Much like how a person pushes themselves during high-intensity exercise training, try to set up money-saving exercises in the same manner. Challenge yourself to save as much as possible within short periods of time by starting small and working your way up. In the event you cannot figure it out by yourself, ask a trusted family member or friend who has been successful at managing their money. I would not advise a person to take money advice from their broke family members and friends. However, even then, the lesson to learn is what not to do.

Developing strong money management skills can help you use the money you have today to live the life you want tomorrow.

I find it a bit different today than in the days of old. Back then, even when people did not have very much, families shared what they had. At a minimum, you could always find something to eat at the neighbor's home. If they had it, everyone was welcome to be a partaker. Nowadays, you hardly know your neighbor, who lives only a few feet away. The most you will get is a quick greeting or smile, and then you each retreat to your corners, not to be seen for days.

As a parent, you always want your children to do better than you and go further than you have. So, why not teach them about managing their money, beginning at an early age? Teach them to be a good steward over what they have, versus worrying about what they do not have. Letting them be a part of creating the family budget not only allows them to feel included in the daily family decisions, but it also shares with them a life principle they will never forget.

While there are no "magic formulas" that guarantee financial success, there are techniques and tips that have proven to be successful. For starters, it begins with the parents, what they were taught, and their current attitudes concerning money.

Are you a good steward of the money that you possess?

Do you have a workable budget, or do you spend, spend, spend every dollar, even before you get it?

Checking your own beliefs about money will help you formulate a basis for managing money.

During my early days, when I stepped out on my own and did not have too much responsibility, I made two mistakes that caused moderate financial setbacks. Fortunately, each instance did not last too long, and they were not so bad that I could not dig myself out and fully recover. In silencing my better judgment, I made two impulse purchases when I should have waited another eight months to a year each time. Looking back, both incidents were teaching moments that forced me to shift my thinking and develop better financial strategies, especially as it related to spending more time in the planning stage.

Once you make a major purchase, you are stuck with your decision, regardless of whatever else is going on. If things get tight, the payment is still due. Financial setbacks will humble you. Hopefully, lessons are learned along the way. Even if it takes a few times before you get it right, do what you can to get your financial affairs in order and try not to make the same mistake too many more times. Consider taking a long look at your decision-making process. Do not forget to ask for help from someone you trust. In addition, when we make mistakes, never forget God's grace and mercy!

I shared my early financial mistakes with my children so that they will think twice before they make similar mistakes. In my sharing, it also let them know I am not Superman; I am not without flaws. Admittedly, they do not always like to hear what I have to say. However, after I break it down, they fully understand why I present other options before they make final decisions. Sometimes, it boils down to a simple accounting problem of income versus liabilities. Once they have a grasp of the numbers, I just sit back and let them make their own decisions. There have been a few times when I thought they did not "get it," but after a good night's sleep, I am proud to say that over the years, they have made rather good decisions — and that is enough to make any parent proud!

Imagine if your parents would have taught you more about money management. If they had, I am sure you would have made a few different choices along the way. Depending on your family's situation during those times, I bet they did the best they could with what they had.

TERRACE V. WHTIE

When I was growing up, I do not remember my grandparents or anyone else ever talking about money. I do not know if that was because they did not have any, or they just did not have the knowledge to share. We could have been living below the poverty line, but as a kid, I had no worries at all and never felt there was a financial squeeze on the family. What I do know with surety is that we had each other and a lot of love. Therefore, in my mind, we were extremely wealthy!

As stated, back in the day, information was not readily available like it is today. I do recall that we received government assistance that helped to supplement the abundance of food that grew in our garden. The assistance seemed to have filled the gaps between paydays. Without it, I am sure things would have been a bit different. While we may not have had a lot of money, we seemed to have everything we needed to survive.

Today, I make sure to share the knowledge I have learned about managing money with my children, to include the money mistakes I have made over the years. One mistake I made was not educating myself early on when I did not have a host of responsibilities. As a matter of fact, I did not even know how money and debt worked. I spent what I wanted when I wanted and did not think long-term.

I distinctly remember paying my credit card bill late — not because I did not have the money to pay it, but because I mailed the payment the day before it was due. That happened not one, not two, but **three times.** Needlessly, I ended up paying a $35.00 late fee each time. As a result, the interest rate also skyrocketed without warning. That did not sit well with me, but I had no one to blame but myself.

After making reckless transactions during the 1980s, I slowly but surely began to pay attention and educate myself on financial matters. During the late 1990s, I was blessed with a great supervisor, who was a financial wizard. During our lunch breaks, he often shared financial tips, such as mastering the financial vocabulary and how to invest in mutual funds. Those tips put me on the right track. I still use them today and share them with my children.

Another vital area I made sure my children were made aware of is **tithing**. Tithing is a concept and biblical directive that commands us to give ten percent of what we earn to God. It is freely given for our increase and not because God needs it. Obedience to giving will open the floodgates to your receiving. The more you give, the more you receive. Conversely, the more you receive, the more you can give. To me, this area of life is crystal clear. Either you believe and abide by it, or you do not.

I must admit that I did not always believe in tithing. As a matter of fact, I started giving regularly and then stopped for no real reason other than I wanted to make unnecessary purchases. In my mind, I could pay cash for the items I wanted versus putting them on credit or waiting until I saved the amount of money needed. Well, needless to say, that was not a good idea because, during that period in time, it seemed that the bottom dropped out of my finances, leaving too many dark days between my basic needs and the next payday. As each day passed, the money I had in my savings account sifted like sand in an hourglass. However, once I started praying, believing, and tithing again, the financial blessings poured in…*again*. Soon, my accounts overflowed, which allowed me to give even more.

Over the years, I have been an avid giver, to include being a good tipper at restaurants. In the early 2000s, I do recall falling victim to the devil and his tactics a second time. I got this not-so-brilliant idea to test God and see if the tithing command really, really worked. Based on my previous debacle, I should have learned a valuable lesson. Although I did not spend the money, I stopped giving it to the local place where I worshipped. Again, my bank account suddenly sprung a leak, looking like an out-of-control sprinkler head. That crazy idea to test God hurt more than my ego and cost me more than I could have imagined. From that point on, I decided to be obedient and give. To this day, I have never looked back.

The tithing concept and biblical command may be hard to believe, but I can personally testify that it has been tried and proven true. Now, I will say that convincing someone that they should give their hard-earned money away may be a difficult task. However, living by example may make it a little easier to show them the way versus just telling them. To make it plain, I tell my children it is all about their level of faith and what they believe.

Once you have the tithing concept down and put it into practice, you will see you have more to **save**, **spend**, and **invest**, and can **create wealth** for generations to come.

"Poor Me" Syndrome

Okay. So, you find yourself smack dab in the middle of parenthood. You may be single, confused, and unsure of what to do or how to proceed in tackling the mountain of parental tasks. After all, there are no pause buttons, no instructions, and no carefully laid out guidelines for you to follow. It may appear that things are falling apart all around you. Bill collectors are constantly nipping at your feet like alligators, your family and best friend are getting on your last nerve, and, as you try to juggle the chainsaw of your job in one hand and the children in the other, you may want to throw your hands in the air and give up. Believe me: I completely understand the pressure and the dilemma.

While all of that may seem overwhelming, remember that it is only a season in your life. The way you respond to circumstances during those times will dictate how long the season lasts and impact the overall outcome. The quicker you recognize it for what it is, assign meaning, and slowly start to change your mindset of the circumstances, the better. You may have to reach out to those same family and friends who are getting on your last nerve for help or advice. Once you get out of your feelings and take yourself out of the mix, you will begin to see your way through and on the other side of the problems. I know that sounds easier said than done, but it can be accomplished with a little faith and practice.

One thing you cannot do is fall into the ***"Poor Me" Syndrome.*** Adverse circumstances may come in threes or even fours, but do not let them create a bottomless pit or endless rut, leading you to believe there is no way out.

As a single father, I went through several trying times. Some were of my own doing, while others were what I now call 'life lessons that propelled me to the next level.' To be honest, I never asked God, *"Why me?"* when it came to the role of being a single father. Instead, I embraced it and thought of it as a blessing. It never crossed my mind that I could not handle it because, most of the time, I maintained a "can-do" attitude. I did not dwell on how I got there and did not overthink simple things. Most importantly, I always believed that God would provide any and everything I needed at the exact time I needed them. It was that confidence that encouraged me to keep my head up, to keep striving, to keep moving forward, and to keep dreaming.

When you think about how fast the world around you moves, you cannot afford to let circumstances get you down because they change faster than the weather or in a nanosecond. If I told you that life would never throw you a wicked sinking curveball, I would be lying to you. Things such as an unexpected pregnancy, a separation, a break-up, a divorce, and even death can put you in unfamiliar territory, causing you to have to make quick decisions.

In addition, you may unexpectedly find yourself in the single-parent swim lane, stroking against the strong undercurrent of life. Like any long-distance swimmer knows, the key is to relax, breathe correctly, find your rhythm, and pace yourself. When it comes to parenting, there is no competition and no records to break. Therefore, when things get a little rough, and you get tired and weary, depend on God's promises, stop paddling, and just float. You will quickly realize that the symptoms of the **"Poor Me" Syndrome** will eventually go away.

PARENTING MEMOIR

Trials Do Not Mean Failures

As a single father, my faith has been tested countless times over the years and will likely be tested in the future. However, my faith is what keeps me moving forward. I admit that there were times when I felt invincible. Other times, I foolishly thought I was a complete failure. Overall, each experience reshaped my thought process and helped me grow as a person and as a father. Through it all, I determined it is helpful to limit or eliminate negative thinking at all costs, manage my discouragement, and never give up!

One of my most challenging times was the year my son spent as a 7th-grader (it must have been a mixture of attending a new middle school and the emotional rollercoaster of the pre-teen years). It was truly a trying time for both of us as he straddled the fence of childhood and adolescence. I stressed the importance of receiving a formal education and tried to ensure that some form of expanding his thinking was incorporated into our daily activities. Often, I would cleverly figure out a way to weave Reading, Science, Social Studies, English, Math, Art, and PE (Physical Education) into our conversations, either during meals or while we were simply looking for socks to match his outfit for the next school day.

You should have seen some of the looks I got when I would ask, *"So, what did you learn in school today?"* or inquire about a specific school project. Sometimes, I got the ***"Oh-here-we-go-again!"*** look, while other times, I got the ***"How'd-you-know-about-that?"*** look. Each time, it was truly a look of amazement—a rarity for my son's face. It sometimes reached up and smacked me in the face as well. It is not that I was surprised by his excitement, quick wit, or precise answers; it's more that I was amazed by his ability to turn it on and off when he wanted to. That translated to letting me know he could do the work...*when he **wanted** to.* The challenge was getting him to see the importance of consistently reading, completing his homework, doing his classwork, and participating in special projects for extra credit.

Like most kids—especially pre-teen boys—my son would rather go outside and ride his bike, skateboard, and play ball (or some other rough and tough extreme sport), instead of picking up a book. Outside activities are encouraged, but I had to set limits often and regulate the time spent on those activities, to include taking more drastic measures when needed. In our home, the power of the belt was always the last resort but could always be moved up on the list of options. Most of the time, a slight change in the tone of my voice was enough to change bad behaviors.

Another area that is near and dear to my heart is being neat and clean. It appears that for many teens, cleaning is thought of as something parents were put on this earth to do. In their mind, parents are to work all day and then come home, cater to their every need, and constantly pick up after them.

Let *THAT* sink in for a moment!

Guess what? That is not the way most parents run their households. Children should be charged with completing chores around the house, based on their capabilities. The older they get, the more chores they should have to complete, or the bigger the tasks should be. Their maturity level should also play into what duties they are given. As they get older, you should have a pretty good idea of what they can do successfully without intervention. Even if they fail or do not complete tasks in the way you want, the idea is for them to learn to be responsible and realize how their decisions impact the entire family.

The challenges mentioned are in no way a complaint about my responsibilities as a single father. In reality, I found it quite rewarding and wish other fathers would step up to the plate and be more involved in fulfilling their parenting duties.

One thing to keep in mind is that when you step up to the plate, it does not mean you are going to hit a home run every time. As you probably know, life will sometimes throw you curveballs that will cause you to take big swings that are totally out of your comfort strike zone. Often, no matter how hard you swing, you find yourself feeling somewhat defeated as you walk back to the dugout with your head hung low, kicking dust. Your mind tells you to position yourself at the end of the bench away from everyone. Being alone to gather your thoughts is not a bad thing when you use the time as an opportunity to regroup and gather your thoughts. You think about how hard you have trained over the years and how you initially made the team. At one point, you were even named team captain and have been the "Most Valuable Player" for many years.

So, as the leader and captain of your family's team, get back into the game with a new "can-do" attitude. As a matter of fact, your time is now! You are next at bat!

PARENTING MEMOIR

The Vow

During a traditional wedding ceremony, a vow is made between two people as an oath, solemn promise, or personal commitment to remain caring, loving, and faithful to each other, all while seeking God's blessing.

If we apply that same thought process to parenting, you will see a similar oath between two people as well. In that case, the oath is between the parent and child, with the child being God's blessing.

Imagine the ceremonial process beginning when the mother becomes pregnant or with the actual physical birth of the child. During that intimate process, the mother forms an unbreakable bond with the child that is much stronger than anything you can think of, except for the love of God. Whether the parent recites a vow aloud in front of an audience or not, they are still biologically, physically, and spiritually forever joined to the child.

Let us take a closer look at the traditional wedding vows. While the actual words may vary, an example of the first line of the traditional vow usually reads something like this:

"I, <u>bride/groom's name</u>, take thee, <u>bride/groom's name</u>, to be my <u>wife/husband</u>, and before God and these witnesses, I promise to be a faithful and true <u>wife/husband</u>."

Now, when we replace the bride and groom's name with the parent and child's name, it would read as follows:

"I, <u>parent's name</u>, take thee, <u>child's name</u>, to be my <u>son/daughter</u>, and before God and these witnesses, I promise to be a faithful and true <u>mother/father</u>."

Keeping with the same thought process, the second and third lines of the traditional vow could read as:

"Will you, <u>bride/groom's name</u>, have <u>bride/groom's name</u> to be your <u>wife/husband</u>? Will you love <u>her/him</u>, comfort and keep <u>her/him</u>, and forsaking all others, remain true to <u>her/him</u> for as long as you both shall live?" ("I will.")

Although a child does not have the option or luxury to choose their parents, if the bride/groom's name is replaced with the child's name, it would read as follows:

"Will you, parent's name, have child's name to be your daughter/son? Will you love her/him, comfort and keep her/him, and forsaking all others, remain true to her/him as long as you both shall live?" ("I will.")

The second to the last line of the vow typically involves the exchanging of rings between the new bride and groom. That exchange is a visible symbol of the promises the couple has made and represents the commitment they have to each other. In the eyes of God, they are now one.

Similarly, in the relationship between a parent and child, imagine the rings being replaced with endless and unconditional love. There are no visible symbols (i.e., an exchange of rings). There are, however, the sparkle of joy in the eyes of the parent at the very first sight of their child, coupled with a big, goofy smile on their face — a moment that is simply priceless.

By now, the picture of the marriage and the meaning of the unspoken vow between a parent and child should be crystal-clear. However, if it is not, the last line of the marriage vow sums it up without a doubt:

"In sickness and in health, in poverty or in wealth, 'til death do us part."

We are to love our children through all circumstances. We may not always like or understand their actions, but we are to love them unconditionally… *'til death do us part.*

My ceremony began when I first found out I was going to be a father. Each time, I was extremely excited and a bit nervous at the same time. After I received the news, I was somewhat overcome with emotions. I needed some alone time to process things fully. Immediately, I went into planning mode to ensure everything was in place throughout the months before and after the little bundles of joy entered this world.

For me, there were several other memorable moments throughout the process, with one being when I viewed the ultrasound and saw the movement of the baby for the first time. The second was when I felt the first kick from the mother's womb. While those two moments were memorable, the most remarkable was the birth itself. It blows my mind how a whole, innocent, and sin-free person can develop and survive in such a small space. That is a true testament of God's awesomeness and miraculous power! As well, the cutting of my children's umbilical cords were proud and truly humbling moments.

Although the births of my daughter and son happened ten years apart, each delivery was exciting and a time for celebration.

As a single father, the union between my children and me is stronger than ever. The bond is solid, and the unconditional love is the driving force way beyond "'til death do us part." I have heard the horror stories of children "divorcing" their parents. Emancipated children become legally responsible for themselves, and the parents are no longer charged as "guilty" for their children's adverse actions. I realize that certain situations may cause children and parents to become estranged, such as abuse and neglect, but a total divorce should proceed with caution. It is necessary to convince a court that the children will benefit from that action, and that separation is the only practical solution. Therefore, it is my prayer that the family would be able to resolve any issues that arise without getting the court system involved.

Medical Emergencies Do Happen

Over the past 20 years or so, the number of single-parent homes has been on the rise. Some may argue that having two parents in the home is always better than having one. For the most part, there are advantages to a well-functioning home where both biological parents are present.

However, if you find yourself in a single-parent role, there may be numerous situations you just cannot handle by yourself. For example, girls often experience things that require a mother's advice or a gentle touch. Now, I am **not** saying a father cannot help daughters maneuver through those challenges, but there is nothing quite like a mother's calming voice in those times of need. Along the same lines, a boy needs his father to be present and active in his life. The father brings a different perspective and manly advice to the table. If both biological parents are actively engaged, it is much easier to count on the other person to take up the slack or carry the entire load if needed. For example, with two parents, they can take turns getting up during the middle of the night with a sick child or develop a schedule to ensure the child's needs are met.

If your family's dynamics do not lend it to uphold the traditional family setup, the responsibilities remain the same and do not go away. Your children still have the same wants and needs. Therefore, you must do what it takes to get the job done. Single-parenthood is not all gloomy, though. Countless children were raised in a single-parent home and went on to be successful.

After a long day at the office, being stuck in traffic, sports practice, preparing dinner, and ensuring homework was complete, I found myself getting up three to four times a night. My body and mind became like a patriot missile, ready to shoot down the slightest sound of a cough, sneeze, or runny nose. I was on an automatic timer and woke up from the deepest sleep (or what I thought was a deep sleep, after only five minutes of closing my eyes) at the slightest hint of any noise. Some call it a "Mother's Instinct." In my case, it was a "Father's Instinct."

When you are a single parent, the child's way to recovery and overall wellbeing rests solely on your shoulders. From time to time, you may consider soliciting help from family members, friends, or support groups. That requires you to recognize and admit that you cannot do it all by yourself. Falling on your knees and praying to God for support and direction are always options and should probably be your first option versus the last. It will help fill any voids or shortcomings you think you may have. In my experience, prayer works 100% of the time, is fail-proof, and is my "get out of jail" card.

Around the age of two, we noticed my son became restless throughout the night. During the same time of the year, he would catch colds, get the sniffles, and suffer from ear infections at the drop of a hat. He was most affected by the change in weather during the Spring and Fall months. After months and months of tests, different medications, and sleepless nights, he was finally diagnosed with asthma.

If you suspect your child has asthma, please pay close attention to the warning signs such as wheezing, coughing, and shortness of breath. Please take it seriously! With the right medication and elimination of the triggers, asthma can be managed over time. Moreover, there is a chance that the symptoms will disappear (even temporarily) as your child gets older. As they age, watch out for asthma-like symptoms to make sure it is not some other condition like bronchitis or pneumonia.

One of my scariest episodes as a single father occurred during May of 2004.

PARENTING MEMOIR

That day, I noticed my son did not want to go outside and did not want anything to eat, which let me know he was not feeling well. I was used to him being highly active and into every extreme sport you can imagine, such as doing backflips off the steps, playing Evil Knievel on his bike, and trying to land every skateboard trick in the book. Instead, on that day, he was laid out across the bed like a new suit before Easter Sunday service. I checked his temperature a couple of times, which started at 100 degrees, quickly elevated to 102 degrees, and seemed to be climbing. I began to worry because I had exhausted my limited medical knowledge and comforting techniques. During that time, I was unfamiliar with Internet searches such as WebMD's portal to look up health information. Therefore, I relied on prayer and the medical information passed down from my grandparents.

As the next couple of hours went by, I noticed he was less and less responsive to anything I tried and to the sound of my voice. It was at that time I realized he needed immediate professional medical attention. Fortunately, we lived less than five minutes away from one of the major hospitals in the area. When we got into the emergency room, the technicians could tell my son was very ill. They **immediately** rushed him to the back and triaged him. Once I informed them that he was asthmatic, they began checking his oxygen level and eventually gave him oxygen. By the next morning, the doctors determined he had pneumonia and stated that had I been a couple of hours late in bringing him to the hospital, his lungs would have probably collapsed. *Just the **thought** of that happening caused me to send up a barrage of prayers of thanks.*

Because he was such a young age and had both asthma and pneumonia, my son was at a higher risk for something unspeakable happening. It was truly a blessing to know the hospital had some of the latest and cutting-edge technology.

During the middle of the night, he was awakened between his short naps to take medication and to undergo high-frequency chest wall oscillation sessions that involved an inflatable vest attached to a machine. The machine mechanically performed chest physical therapy by vibrating at a high frequency to thin and loosen the mucus. The vibrating vest they put on my son looked more like a torture chamber used on prisoners of war, primarily since it was being used on a child.

The next couple of days and nights brought on more medication, oscillating sessions, and fervent praying. My son soon began to show some improvement and was eventually released from the hospital. What started as a quick trip to the emergency room turned into a five-day stay in the hospital.

After that rememberable event, I educated myself on how to manage the asthma disease. I also had to talk to my son about the disease so that he would know how to recognize the onset of the symptoms. Over the years, his symptoms have become less intense, and he no longer takes preventative medication. However, we continue to remain keenly aware of and keep a watchful eye on the asthma triggers during the Spring and Fall months.

Overcoming Misunderstood Behavior

Attention-Deficit Hyperactivity Disorder (ADHD) is a condition that typically shows up in a child's early years of school. The *principal* characteristics of ADHD are **inattention**, **hyperactivity**, and **impulsivity**. Usually, it is hard for children with the condition to control their behavior or pay attention for an extended period.

According to a national 2016 parent survey, the Center for Disease Control and Prevention estimates the number of children ever diagnosed with ADHD is 6.1 million, with the majority being children ages 6-11 years old. Some children may display ADHD symptoms but at an extremely low level. That is why children need to receive a thorough examination from a well-qualified professional.

While seeking medical help is extremely important, parents should be aware that children are sometimes **misdiagnosed** as having ADHD. In my case, my son was diagnosed with the condition after sporadic inattentiveness in school. For the life of me, I could not figure out what was going on inside his brain. After all, I was supposed to be "Superdad" and should have had all the answers. I took pride in being able to analyze a problem and devise a solution quickly, yet I found myself a bit stumped and without an explanation. I thought to myself, *"How could such a good kid cause so much havoc in all his classes and show no signs of the condition at home?"* The reports from his teachers included descriptions such as "disruptive" and "not working to his full potential."

That misbehavior went on for almost a year and a half. Over time, it took its toll on the teachers, me as the parent, and eventually, my son. I could tell he was getting frustrated and tired of having to sit in the corner during class time. I had to constantly remind him of how he should conduct himself as a young man, especially in a controlled environment. I was also aware that it was important not to stifle his creativity as he developed and learned his own individuality.

Depending on a person's frame of reference and outlook, clichés such as *"Boys will be boys"* and *"It takes a little longer for boys to mature than girls"* could contain an ounce of truth. Still, knowing the importance of maintaining self-control and the consequences of not controlling himself in class is also a part of his life education.

With the high student-teacher ratio, most teachers do not have the time to deal with an inattentive or disruptive child—

at least not for an extended period. After all, teachers usually have a strict curriculum and 25 to 30 other students who demand their attention. A lot of teachers will bend over backward to help the students who show potential and an eagerness to learn, but a disruptive student will rarely gain their long-term support. Once the student displays what is perceived as a repeated negative behavior, it forces the teacher to take alternative actions. Depending on the situation, that action can be looked upon as either positive or negative.

During my son's 3rd-grade year of school, one of his teachers told him that although a 'C' is not a *failing* grade, it was still a ***good*** grade. I interpreted that to mean the teacher telling him he should strive to obtain a grade of 'C' and be okay with it. Her comment enraged me, and I immediately requested a parent-teacher conference. I wanted to understand her train of thought as she made such comments to her students. I cannot clearly recall all that she said during our meeting, but I do know it was not good enough. Neither was it on any list of excuses she could have provided. Imagine putting a student in a box, closing the lid, and taping it shut. Basically, that teacher liked to tell her students, *"This is all you will ever achieve, so get comfy with it!"* I wonder how often those types of comments are uttered by other teachers.

To me, that was a confidence killer for not only my son but for all young children who heard those words. It took me about two years to erase that negativity from my son's little brain while replacing it with positive and encouraging messages. Even to this day, my son will try to play that card when he does not want to do his work or try his very best. However, the Big Joker card is quickly pulled from his card deck of life and is replaced with nothing but Aces.

A key milestone or turning point for us happened one day when I heard my son say, *"I can do it when I want to."* It was as if a lightbulb turned on inside my head. That was all I needed to hear. That comment led to an immediate change in strategy and my overall approach in the way I assisted with his homework and providing day-to-day instructions. From that moment on, there was a noticeable positive change in his grades and overall attitude toward achieving and being his best.

How amazing was it that such a simple lesson would have such an impact on an outcome?! I wondered who learned the biggest lesson; my son or me?

After some time, there was a long break from any ADHD symptoms. However, I noticed the inattentiveness and hyperactivity resurfaced. Being that it was his first year of high school, his ability to focus and learn more of the basics was imperative. The experiences learned during his Freshman year would help to catapult him into his Sophomore, Junior, and Senior years.

As a parent, you want to do all you can to ensure your child succeeds in all areas of life. Often, children are labeled as lazy, stubborn, and unwilling to learn—especially young males. In our case, I knew that was not true. I knew I needed to try another approach. I needed to think outside of the box. Therefore, I agreed to a prescription of a low-dose medication on a trial basis. That was a difficult decision, but it was one made after a lot of research and prayer.

If you find yourself in a similar situation, consider talking to a physician—preferably a specialist—whom you trust and only after having exhausted all other resources. Do not be afraid to ask relatives, friends, coworkers, and support groups for assistance if you are unsure of what to do. Educate yourself as much as possible regarding any medication the doctor may consider administering to your child. By doing so, you will be able to assist your child throughout the process and ease both of your minds.

After I conducted thorough research and determined that medication was the best course of action for my son, I located a trustworthy physician who prescribed the medication. As reluctantly as I was about medicating my son, I concluded I was doing the best thing for him.

The first couple of days were nerve-racking because I did not know what to expect, especially with so many potential side effects. Every person that takes any medication responds differently, so there was a legitimate cause for concern. When I talked to my son about the medicine, I made sure I kept it as simple as possible without a lot of medical terminologies. I explained his behavior, why he had to take the medication, and what to do when I was not around—just in case he ran into problems. Taking those steps helped us both to manage his condition. Soon, his negative behaviors turned into positive ones.

Protect the Mind

A "cliché" is a phrase or opinion that is often overused and portrays a lack of original thought. For example, you might have heard the old cliché, *"A mind is a terrible thing to waste."* While that saying may be overused, there may be some truth to it.

The human mind is a massive tissue that acts like a mega computer, but its capacity is much greater than any computer in the world. Think about it: **It was the human mind that conceived and built the computer!** The mind controls everything you do and the things you do not. Everything that you imagine and do starts in the mind with a stimulus response-type of action. Therefore, you should guard the traffic that flows in and out of your mind to preserve and protect it.

As an adult, things I have read, heard, seen, and focused on have impacted my decisions. Now, take just a moment to envision the delicate and fragile mind of an innocent child and how things that are read, heard, seen, and focused on impact their mind. Since parents act as the gatekeeper, we must filter and control what seeps into their mind, which, in turn, will help regulate what comes out.

PARENTING MEMOIR

Today, children have more access to things that can pollute their minds—much moreso than I had when growing up. Consider for just a moment the lyrics of the hottest song of the Summer. Then, add the video that complements that song, all while giving an explicit visual of the unimaginable. For the most part, song lyrics have drastically changed over the years (some would argue for the worst). The sign of the times has turned what used to be songs of love and the simple things of life into songs about hate, murder, money, guns, and foul language.

Take this time to step outside of your normal thinking and look at the effects music can have on the mind. With a positive spin, music has proven to cause a relaxed state of mind in both infants and adults. Soothing music is often played to quiet agitated babies or adults who have just finished a hectic day or workweek. In stark contrast, loud music or music with negative lyrics have proven to cause the total opposite reaction. Instead of reducing agitation, it can cause unrest, increase a person's heart rate, and can even impede a child's learning ability over time.

While it is impossible to totally eliminate negative input into the mind from music, TV shows, or other images, it is possible for parents to improve communication about that negativity with their children. Strive to talk to them about what they are listening to, watching on TV, or browsing while on the Internet.

Today's youth appear to be both blessed and cursed at the same time. They are blessed by being technologically savvy but, in many cases, seem to be cursed by that same blessing. They have immediate access to tons of information right at their fingertips. It only takes a slip of the finger to be one number or letter off from an intended website, and children could find themselves in a deep and dark world — one that they may not be knowledgeable enough about to get out of. Therefore, ensure they are aware of the possible pitfalls. Also, you may want to consider setting parental controls on the TV and the Internet as extra precautions.

Another thing to look at when you are trying to prevent negative input from entering your child's mind is your contribution. There are some parents who — *whether deliberately or subconsciously* — deposit bits of negativity into their child's mind. That input can slowly destroy their self-esteem or hinder them from reaching their full potential. Often, parents push their children to be something they are not or do not want to do. Some parents might argue that they want their children to succeed and have more than they did when they were growing up. That goal is all well and good. However, when we peel back the onion and look at each layer individually, the real reasons are exposed as to why some parents have that narrow view.

One possible conclusion is because parents want to live out their dreams or failed attempts vicariously through the children. For example, some parents did not have the chance to attend college, did not open that business they dreamed of, or did not pursue other lifelong dreams. **Remember: Those were *your* dreams.** It is not your child's fault that you did not achieve them. Do not saddle your children with your guilt or baggage. Allow them to be free to develop and live their own dreams.

Peer pressure can also have a significant impact on your child's outlook and success. Your child is often exposed to things you may consider much too adult for their virgin eyes and ears. You should be aware of who is hanging around your child and, if possible, get to know their parents well. Let us face it: Most children are curious and may not have a keen understanding of unhealthy relationships and situations. The very things you have warned them about are what attracts their attention. A simple dare from one of their friends can turn into a lifetime of trouble and turn the whole family dynamic upside down if left unchecked.

Realistically, it is impossible to control whom your child befriends. Communication between parent and child is the key. One way to potentially cut down on some of the negativity that enters your child's mind is to simply talk to them and set guidelines—not just when something goes wrong, but also when things are going well. Without communication, by the time the parent determines something is wrong, it would likely be late in the game. By then, you would likely want to beat up everyone in the house (including yourself) for not paying attention to the missed red flags.

PARENTING MEMOIR

Time Waits for No One

As a parent, it is imperative that you spend time with your children. I am not talking about just any old time, between time, or in the meantime. I am referring to real **quality time**. I define quality time as that special time set aside for your children to develop and improve your overall relationship with them, to build their self-esteem, and to give them something that they will always remember and cherish. They really do not care if you have a busy schedule; they just want to spend time with you.

Contrary to popular belief, children are easy to please. It is not **always** about the latest video game, cell phone, gadget, a pair of sneakers, or even a trip around the world. The things they really want do not cost you a thing, such as giving them more attention, engaging in a meaningful conversation, assuring them they are loved no matter what, and showering them with hugs and kisses when they are feeling down or for no apparent reason whatsoever. Try having a simple conversation when they are **NOT** told what to do (i.e., clean up their room, pick up toys, let down the toilet seat). Sometimes, a little hug often does the trick. Saying *"I love you"* runs long and deep and works wonders. Just think: If your children hear those words from you daily, it will build their confidence and overall trust in you. When they get older, it will be easier for them to express the same to their spouse, children, significant other, and real friends throughout their lives.

I have learned my son is fascinated by stories about my childhood. We often discuss the things I liked, disliked, and did as a kid. I tell stories about shooting marbles, hunting, fishing, kicking a football, playing basketball, and riding one of my several handmade bicycles until dark almost every day of the week. The joy of watching his eyes light up in disbelief is priceless. Even now, we talk about developing traditions of our favorite pastimes, so that he can share them with his children and grandchildren one day.

Often, extra money is hard to come by in a single-parent household. It seems like money plays a no-win game of hide-and-seek, or it sifts through your pockets as if there is a bottomless pit. However, there are countless activities you can do with your children that will not cost a dime or break the bank. It will only cost you a little of your time…and it will be time well spent, I might add! Based on the proven rate of return on that type of investment, it is a no-brainer that it is wise to invest your time on that sure bet.

Some suggestions include:

- Taking a long walk in the park or a short walk down the street. Not only is taking a walk a good bonding activity, but it also has health benefits as well. You burn calories, lose weight, and your overall immune system and mood will improve.
- A good piggyback ride will always tickle their fancy and will make anyone smile, even other adults.
- Watching your child do tricks and flips is always fun. Even if you know the tricks they are attempting have no chance of working at all, it is a way to let them know that what they do matters to you. It is knowing they have your undivided attention that truly counts.
- Allow them to help prepare a meal without criticizing or worrying about the mess they may make. You never know; you just might be prepping the next Food Channel Network star!
- Play a game of indoor or outdoor hide-and-seek with your children.
- Watch their favorite TV show with them.
- Give them free rein to do whatever they would like for a couple of hours, providing it is safe. That will, of course, require a few ground rules and guidelines you both can live with after fun time is all over.

Whatever activities you choose to do, time and timing are everything. After all, none of us will be around forever, so spending quality time with your children now is extremely important. Consider this: As you think about the events that have occurred during your lifetime to date, time sure flies!

Knowing what you want, staying focused, and remaining grounded are all keys to your future success. At the time this book is being written, I have a little over two years before I am eligible for full retirement from my current job. Although I can retire at any time before then, there would be a hefty cost for not waiting until the time served and age retirement requirements are met. I must admit that I am ready to leave corporate America to see what the next chapter in my life has to offer, as well as write a few chapters of my own. It is a little scary, but I am excited about the unknown and countless new opportunities! As a matter of fact, I am *SO* excited, I have placed an app on my cell phone that is actively counting down the time to the very last second when I become fully eligible to retire!

One early morning while lying in my bed, I found myself staring at the retirement countdown clock tick away as several things crossed my mind. I began to think about how blessed I was to have had such enjoyable and prosperous careers — one completely done, and another one on the way just around the corner. I also thought about the millions of people who did not have the same opportunities I had and will have to work their entire lives to make ends meet. Over the years, I have often thought about why it seems as if some people are more blessed than others.

For a moment, negative thoughts tried to enter my mind and take up residence. When they showed up, they bought with them the designer luggage of guilt riding shotgun in the passenger's seat. I quickly remembered that although they show up, negative thoughts and guilt were not invited into my world. Needless to say, they were not-so-kindly tossed out of my peaceful space.

As each second ticked away on the retirement clock, I found myself also thinking about the amount of time I have left here on this earth. I can choose to do good for my children (and people, in general), or I can sit idle and squander time away, never to get that time back. While no one knows their appointed time, everyone should realize that they do have the same appointment...just at a *different* time.

A few years ago, I had a conversation with my son as he was trying to navigate life and plan his future on his own.

While those efforts are admirable, he quickly realized that without the proper guidance and tools, his internal navigation system kept telling him to keep straight, take unfamiliar exits, and recalculate his plans. As a parent, I have traveled down some of those same roads he attempted to go down or avoid altogether. However, there is nothing like experiencing things for yourself. As painful as it was for me at times to see him bump his head time and again, I purposefully remained silent…most of the time. My silence was not to be confused with, *"I told you so."* Rather, he was afforded opportunities to learn from his mistakes. By the grace of God, none of his mistakes were life-ending or self-esteem shattering. His journey has been a true learning experience for both of us.

As an exercise, I printed out an image of two feet on a piece of paper. The image consisted of a bare left foot and a bare right foot, standing side by side. I then placed the sheet of paper on the floor in my formal dining room, which is rarely used. The paper was positioned directly underneath the large double-sized window. From that window, there is a clear view of the driveway, mailbox, neighbors, birds, butterflies, flowers, bicycle riders, and a few cars that venture into the cul-de-sac. I told my son to replace those images that are easily seen through the window with tasks and opportunities in life, such as:

- Traveling outside of the place where he grew up.
- Watching the sunrise and sunset.
- Getting a good education.
- Acquiring a job that pays well enough to build wealth.
- Spending quiet time getting to know himself better.
- Knowing what he likes and dislikes.
- Building a relationship with God.
- Falling in love.
- Conquering fears.
- A host of other available opportunities that so many others walk past or take for granted.

I then said to him, *"All those things are great and achievable, but if you are not dedicated or take steps to achieve those things, you will be standing at that window looking at not only life passing you by, but also at the achievements of others."*

Three years later, that same piece of paper with the image of bare feet is still on the floor of my formal dining room underneath the window. That is intended to serve as a reminder for both him and me to keep dreaming, believing, striving, and moving forward.

To you, I say: Regardless of the circumstance, step out on faith. Do not let life pass you by. **Time waits for no one.**

Dating

This chapter is not about children. **THIS** section is for an adult or responsible parent who has a desire to "get their groove back."

There is no right or wrong time to get back on the dating scene. It is all up to you and what you feel comfortable doing. In general, dating is a relationship between two people who assess the other's suitability as a prospective partner. The interaction is a form of courtship and can be done alone or in a group setting in which protocol and practices are usually set.

Over time, the adults will determine if they are compatible with one another. Depending on the individual goals—which should be discussed upfront—the couple will decide to continue the relationship as it is or take it to the next level. The latter could mean spending more time together, establishing a committed relationship, or getting engaged and eventually married.

If intimacy is your primary goal, just remember that intimacy is a choice and not a requirement, so choose wisely.

If companionship is your primary goal, then stick to your principles and go for it!

I found that when adults who date are open and completely honest upfront about their intentions, finding a companion can be just as fulfilling and rewarding as a long-term, committed relationship. The key is always to **communicate, communicate, communicate!**

When you are single and have no children, the dating options are wide open. You can go out when you want, where you want, and with whom you want. The only limits are what you decide. However, if establishing a long-term relationship is your goal, take your time finding a compatible person. You can never be 100% sure, but with time, you will have a good idea of precisely what you want, subjects in which you are willing to make compromises, and those areas that are nonnegotiable.

When you have children and decide to step out on the dating scene, things will be a bit different. For starters, your time is not your own. You will not be able to go out whenever you want, go wherever you want, and be in the company of whomever you want. You must always consider your children first, along with how soon you want to introduce another person to the existing family environment. When children are a part of the mix, careful planning must take place in order to have a chance at a successful dating period.

You must also make sure the dynamics of the courtship work for both parties. For example, if you have children and the person you are pursuing does not, it could negatively impact the relationship or the pool of potential candidates. If both of you have children, that could pose an even more challenging situation, especially if they are younger children. Either way, clear communication will go a long way and eliminate unnecessary stress.

Some singles complain and say, *"There are no good women around"* or *"A good man is hard to find."* My perspective is that it depends on how you define "good" and what your goals are. For example, if you view a good man or woman as someone with some of the qualities you desire in a mate, then each person will have a different definition of what "good" means to them. Some of the qualities many singles take into consideration when dating include:

- ➤ Being responsible
- ➤ Being faithful
- ➤ Are physically attractive

- Have a good economic and social status
- Are ambitious and intelligent
- Are genuinely compatible
- Maintain a good sense of stability

That list of qualities is not exhaustive and may not seem like much to ask, but you would be surprised to learn otherwise.

If you have not found the type of person you are looking for, it does not mean they do not exist and that you should settle for anything less than you desire. I must also bring to your attention that our standards are sometimes so high that we miss the person who is truly Godsent. Everyone we meet is not meant to be a doctor, lawyer, or professional athlete. What about that nice person your friend introduced you to? What about that person you have known for a while? What about the man or woman you walk by several times a week, but you choose not to give them the time of day? I do understand that a workplace environment could complicate things and may not be the ideal place to meet someone, but do not rule it completely out. We often say we want and pray for a specific type of person, but when they suddenly appear, we would not know them from a knot on a log.

If you have not found a mate, I am a firm believer in **Matthew 6:33,** which states:

> *"But seek first His kingdom and His righteousness, and all these things will be given to you as well."*

In my opinion, that passage of scripture is plain as day. When you *"seek first His kingdom,"* all things will be given to you, which includes things such as good health, wealth, prosperity, and yes, even a mate—not just any mate or an occasional date, but one who is sent by Almighty God. How do you know he or she is "the one"? How can you be sure? Well, do not be afraid to talk to God about it. Be sure to be as **specific** as possible! Ask God what kind of mate He wants you to have. The old cliché, *"Be careful what you pray for,"* is alive and well. You might just get that person for which you prayed. Let me share an example that might help you better grasp the necessity for specificity when in prayer.

If you just pray for "a man/woman to come into your life," that is exactly what you are going to get: a man or a woman. That man or woman you have cried and prayed for could be as crazy as a box of rocks, but you have yourself "a man" or "a woman" that you prayed for!

Are you that desperate to just settle for something less than you deserve? I would hope not!

Once you have met the person of your dreams, take your time getting to know them. Do not spill all your beans right away. Keep most of them in the bag. In other words, do not tell **ALL** your business from the start. For example, think twice about sharing too much regarding your family's history, medical issues, and finances in the beginning stages. After all, you really do not know that person and will need to decide if they are worth your time. As you get more and more comfortable with the direction things are going, then and only then should you share more.

In addition, pay attention to how much information the other person shares. If you feel they are sharing too much or are being a bit evasive when answering your questions, make a mental note to see how long it continues.

Numerous other yellow flags could turn red in a relatively short time, such as if they can dish out jokes but cannot take one or if they appear to be self-centered or closed-minded to the ideas of others. When attentive to your needs, you will also come to know if the other person is looking for a caretaker, cook, or maid versus a companion. Whenever you get negative vibes during what should be relaxing, fun, and casual conversations, watch out! They are noteworthy indicators because eventually, you must decide if that person is worthy of meeting your children. If not, be okay with telling them the relationship will not work. However, if the person appears to be the type you are looking for, give it a chance. Trust me: As time goes on, you will know that you know.

Granted, there are some things you should not ever compromise—especially those things that are deeply rooted in your belief system. The first thing that comes to mind is your religious beliefs. If your newfound partner does not know who Jesus is and does not have a clue of what is in the Bible, that is probably a flashing neon sign. If you still insist that person is the one for you, understand there may be a few sleepless nights ahead and could be more than you bargained for. The point is you may want to take heed and proceed with caution.

This is not to say that people who have not given their life over to Jesus Christ are not good people. I am saying that if this is a big part of your core belief system, try introducing Jesus through your conversations. Over time, I am sure you will get an idea of where the other person stands on the subject.

While I am not an expert on making choices in a mate (I have made plenty of mistakes along the way), an inconsistency in core religious beliefs can be a deal-breaker.

Okay. So, your new relationship is going well. Everything appears to be working as you had hoped. Now, you must ask yourself, *"Can my new mate really handle the step-role?"* Whether they realize it or not, they just became a stepparent by default. The family dynamics just changed, so it may be a challenge for all parties involved. It is a package deal. Accepting the role of a stepparent requires a committed individual with the ability to give unconditional love and support.

Unfortunately, some single parents become so wrapped up in their newfound partner that they forget the small, important details. Often, they rush into a committed relationship (marriage included) without even knowing much about the other person. Six days, six weeks, or six months of fun and excitement can lead to a world of heartache and pain. That is not to say all fast-moving relationships turn out bad or that there is a magic grace period before a relationship has a chance to succeed. The point here is that it is imperative that you get to know the other person well, especially when children are a part of the equation.

When it comes to dating, it would be irresponsible of me if I did not mention the elephant in the room — the big elephant that no one likes to discuss openly but everyone wants: Sex.

If you believe in the teachings of the Bible about sex before marriage, the preferred actions around this topic are pretty clear. You can simply decide to obey or not obey. Either way, I am not here to judge because, as a single father, I know it is hard to abstain. We must at least try to practice self-control and not self-indulgence. When the road to temptation seems long and overbearing, always remember there are exit ramps such as 1 Corinthians 6:18. I purposely chose not to quote the scripture here because I want to encourage you to explore what God's Word has to say around the subject of sex. After all, you will eventually need to talk to your children about sex and how it can impact their lives, especially if they make the wrong choices. Therefore, why not start with the truth (as told in the Holy Bible) and build your conversation on that foundation?

If true love is what you are seeking, please ensure you have found self-love first. I am not talking about doing so in a narcissistic way, but rather a deeper regard for your own wellbeing and happiness. That may sound strange coming from a man because, as an unspoken "rule," we do not openly talk about self-love as much as we should. In my opinion, men should spend more time exploring that area for their own happiness, just like most women do. Fathers, the more you know about self-love, the better conversations will be with your children—especially your daughters.

Plus, let us face it, fellas: As 45- to 64-year-old middle-aged men, we need to stay on top of our self-love before we attempt to attract a date. You may find your confidence level fluctuating from time to time, but never date below your self-worth. I am sure there will be times when you get rejected, just as there will be other times when you do the rejecting. Be okay with it either way. Do not be devastated. Do not give up trying. Accept it for what it is and keep it moving.

Remember that self-love begins when you see yourself exactly how God sees you. Recognize all that He created you to be.

Lastly, once you are back in the dating game, the same tips you should be giving to your daughters also apply to you, especially if you have been off the scene for a while. Realize things have changed since your early dating years when things appeared to be much simpler. Personally, I do not think it is too much to tell your daughters that if they are going on a date, they should drive their own car (initially), let someone know where they are going, and expect a periodic check-in on them from you. These days, I would go as far as to request they share a picture of their date (preferably a recent photo) — just in case things unexpectedly turn bad. That may sound a bit old-school, but it is better to be safe than sorry. Use your common sense.

PARENTING MEMOIR

Fruit of My Labor

What now seems like many years ago, this parenting book idea first entered my mind like a Category 4 hurricane. At the time, I was focused on writing a book of poetry. After reading the works of poets like Maya Angelou, Langston Hughes, and Nikki Giovanni, I was inspired to test my skills and explain my perspective on various day-to-day situations.

I started to take a closer look at the things around me that probably go unnoticed by most people. I consider myself somewhat of a quiet and extremely observant person with the keen ability to apply an equal and unbiased opinion. Looking deeper than what is on the surface was something I took pride in doing. Therefore, I always try to use my God-given talents to the best of my ability.

Building on inspiration I gained from the journalist and novelist, John Boy Walton from the 1970s drama television series, "The Waltons," I tried to press through several dry spells in my writing.

SIDEBAR: The main story of the show was set in Walton's Mountain, a fictional mountain-area community in fictitious Jefferson County, Virginia, during the Great Depression and World War II. I was impressed by their strong sense of family and John Boy's human-interest stories about faraway places.

There was a period when my brain lacked the stimulation to write. I found myself suffering from a severe case of "writer's block," which is basically when there is a psychological inhibition that prevents a writer from writing. While penning this book, my mind kept wandering away to things I should not have been concerned with, especially in the early stages of writing.

I also adopted a bad habit of editing while writing. Every word or thought had to be in the perfect place the very first time. After hours of proofing my work, I quickly realized that stressing about getting things right the first time was a waste of time because I ended up spending more time rewriting those things I had spent only a few minutes writing to begin with! The lesson learned from that minor setback was to buckle down and write without ceasing and that when the ideas are flowing, just write without concern for grammar or sentence structure.

Several times, I woke up in the middle of the night, thinking about how much I did not want to market the book. I allowed things like participating in a book reveal, Facebook live sessions, and numerous other nightmarish things to creep into my mind. I also thought a lot about getting up in front of a crowd to talk about myself and the content of the book. Remember: I consider myself a very private person, so why would I want to put myself out there to be criticized? Once those negative thoughts took up residence in my mind, my knees began to shake, and doubt crept in.

I realized I had to make changes and regain the momentum that was abruptly halted. I could not afford to lay awake, tossing and turning during the night, all while knowing I had a goal to accomplish.

One of my coping mechanisms was to grab a pen and paper and write in the dark. The room was not pitch black, though. It was dimly lit by the light of the television or the moonlight shining through the open blinds. My point for doing that was not to ruin my eyes, but rather to record those free-flowing ideas that would not go away. Usually, after a 30-minute session of writing in the dark, I would drift off to sleep in a matter of minutes. The real issue was trying to decipher my writing the next day. Often, words were written atop each other, and sentences drifted out of their assigned lane into oncoming traffic. However, after a few minutes of repetitive reading, I was able to get the gist of each thought, as was written in real-time.

After a few consecutive nights of no progress, I decided to return to the source. I recalled several scriptures in the New King James Version of the Bible that I had read numerous times—only that time, I had a better understanding of each passage as they revealed more profound meanings. I suppose that is why the Holy Spirit is known as "The Helper." I liken the experience to getting an adrenaline shot in the arm.

The first scripture I was led to was **Proverbs 16:3:**

> *"Commit your works to the Lord,*
> *and your thoughts will be established."*

That passage spoke to me, encouraging me to continue trusting God like everything depended on Him. I needed to write like everything depended on me.

Other scriptures included **2 Timothy 1:7:**

> *"For God hath not given us the spirit of fear; but of power,*
> *and of love, and of a sound mind."*

And **Habakkuk 2:2:**

"Then the Lord answered me and said, 'Write the vision, and make it plain on tablets, that he may run who reads it.'"

Once I regained my footing, the ideas began to flow freely again, and increased awareness to recommit to God's will allowed me to visualize the endgame and leave the rest to Him. I began to see the fruit of my labor when I really started paying closer attention to the things I had learned over the years and started applying them to my daily activities. More importantly, I saw how the things I have read in the Bible became alive right before my eyes. My understanding and focus became clearer, and I could see the manifestation in my life. I will admit that I did not always pay attention to those powerful and life-changing words, which, in many ways, gave me a fresh outlook as I applied them to my writing. Often, I would insert my name into certain scriptures to make them even more personal. That was the beginning of a new power surge to resume my writing with a vengeance.

More evidence of the fruit of my labor can be seen when I look at how my children's lives are turning out. Anyone with children knows that they sometimes act as if they have selective hearing. It seems like the crystal-clear guidance, multiple recommendations, and late-night talks are all for naught and make you want to pull your hair out! However, most of the time, you find they heard you all along and will usually come around at their own pace. The key is not to give up on them or your ability to help them navigate through life. Things may get rough and rocky from time to time, but remember to find a way to provide guidance and share your ideas with them lovingly.

During one of my Executive Leadership courses, a well-respected retired Vice Admiral (3-stars) from the United States Navy shared a story about leadership that I quickly applied to fatherhood. He used a roll of Lifesavers candy as a prop to say that during a person's career and leadership role, you encounter many different types of people who come from a wide range of backgrounds and experiences. Some of the people and encounters, you may like more than others, but the key is you do not throw them away just because you do not like them. Instead, you should embrace them and share those experiences with others.

Much like a roll of Lifesavers candy, there is usually a wide range of flavors:

- Cherry
- Raspberry

- Watermelon
- Orange
- Pineapple

You may not like them all but take a chance and remember the experience of tasting a new flavor. If you do not like it, do not throw it away the next time you open a new pack; share it with a friend or offer it to a stranger. You never know if it is their favorite and, more importantly, you never know what kind of relationship it may lead to by a simple act of kindness.

That story made me think it could be a simple lesson for parents and children. Think about it: Each parenting situation is different, as well as each child is unique. Of course, you cannot throw children away, and they should not be abandoned. Instead, they should be embraced along with their many differences while sharing your life stories and experiences with them.

Equally as important, be sure to share your parenting tips with other parents who may not be as experienced in certain parenting areas. You never know how a simple Lifesavers candy story can impact another parent and, possibly, the lives of their children.

Life and Death

From the first breath into the nostrils of man, God has provided everything we will ever need to live a fruitful life. Through His endless grace and mercy, we reap benefits such as joy, protection, and provision, and truly marvel at personally knowing and worshipping Him. Regardless of the many circumstances and ups and downs that life may bring, we are to remain faithful. We are to seek Him. We are to choose life and not death.

God calms the many storms of life and blesses us with the desires of our hearts. He rewards us with the precious fruit of the womb: our children. We are to love them, train them, discipline them, and, most importantly, lead them to the Lord. We show them the ins and outs of life based on our experiences. We often map out their lives from the very beginning, from what to eat, what to wear, what time do participate in activities, and where to go. We help choose their friends, career path, type of mate, and even the way they raise their own children.

One subject that is often left off the table of life conversations is death. Just as God breathed that first breath into our nostrils, that last breath marks the end of life as we know it. It is the only appointment that is on our internal calendar that will **never** be late. We all have that same appointment, just on a different date and time. Regardless of today's medical advances, technology, and religion, **no one** knows the *exact* date and time our name will be called. All we know for sure is that it **will** happen.

Some may think that death is a bad thing. After all, it usually comes at the most inopportune time. We like to think we can handle it, but most people are never really prepared. The good thing is that we were never meant to handle death by ourselves. One of the keys is preparation — preparing ourselves for the next life **and** preparing our loved ones for our final departure from this life, especially our children.

It is easy to have "the birds and the bees talk" with your children, but talking about death can be extremely stressful for all parties involved. However, it is a conversation that must take place and will be one of the most challenging yet important conversations you should have with your children. It does not have to be one long conversation. Break it down into many sessions. Depending on the ages of your children, maturity level, and overall responsibility level, you can be creative in your approach. Regardless, that powerful conversation must occur.

As I contemplate the meaning of life, I find myself dissecting the right and wrong things I have done. I think we all can relate to beating ourselves up a few times over something not worth the thought or something we had absolutely no control over. If we had just one more chance to right our wrongs or not go down "that" road, we may have experienced a different outcome. However, there are rarely any do-overs. We make the best of the time we have left, prepare our children for their future, and prepare ourselves for eternity.

I have had several conversations with my children about death and where we go when we die. No matter how hard the brightest minds use the latest drugs to try and prolong our lives or save us, we must understand and accept that inevitable path. Although the conversations about death were a little uncomfortable, they were crucial and necessary. We not only talked about death itself, but also about living our lives to the fullest, the life after death, and preparing children for their parents' deaths (the latter is often left out but is one of the most critical pieces of the conversation). For children to have to think of the adults in their lives whom they have known their entire lives and who have been their solid rock as no longer being around is unimaginable. The idea alone can take a while to process fully and can be downright scary.

I believe that when it comes to death, there is no full recovery from the loss of a loved one. However, to soften the blow, we draw near to God, rely on similar experiences of others, remember the good times, and try to move forward. When relying on the experiences of those who have lost loved ones, be sure not to place your feelings into their box. Know that it is okay to mourn in your own way. Take all the time you need to honor and remember your loved ones.

In my humble opinion, drawing near to God is always the first and best option. Part of what happens when you die depends on what happened when you lived. Therefore, seek God's kingdom first.

At the other end of the spectrum, if you find yourself trying to console someone who has just lost a parent or child, please be careful in the way you deliver your message. Do not try to play God. Instead, carry God in your heart, and He will give you the words of comfort to say.

While we are alive and have a sound mind, there are a few things we can do to ease the pain and burden on our loved ones:

1. **After the conversation about death, develop a plan of action.** As a starting point, consider taking inventory of your belongings, to include minute details such as writing down the model and serial numbers of your electronics and appliances. I would also include their estimated cost in case the insurance company or court system needs that information. Besides, having that type of information readily available could be handy if you needed to replace items through your insurance company for any reason.

   Once your comprehensive list is complete, you will be surprised at the things you have accumulated over the years. It could also be a good time to dispose of items you no longer use or need. After a parent's death, your children will have to go through your belongings anyway, so this step may save some time as well as decrease the grieving period.

   Therefore, while you are alive, why not be in control and dictate what happens to your belongings? It may even be a good idea to include your children in the decision-making while you are alive.

   Remember: The more you can do yourself and take care of while you are alive, the easier it will be on your loved ones.

2. **Another cost-free thing you can do is write down all your account user identifications and passwords.** Of course, they will need to be kept in a secure location with limited access. Let us face it: Most of us have several open accounts. Some, we have completely forgotten about…until we look at our credit report.

This is one area where you may want to consider breaking the rule of never writing down a password. Believe me, I understand that caution, especially with computer hacking and identity theft being at an all-time high. In today's technologically driven world, we have numerous passwords for almost everything. When your loved ones are gone, facial recognition, fingerprints, and other biometrics are not options to access their accounts. Therefore, the next best thing is to consider having a written record of key passwords and telling a trusted family member where they are located. It is also vital to ensure your list of accounts and passwords are periodically updated so that your loved ones will not spend time researching closed accounts and getting locked out of others by trying to use the wrong passwords.

While you are recording that information, do not forget to include the essential day-to-day accounts such as the electric, gas, cable, and phone. They are accounts that can be easily closed online, if needed. Then, move on to your personal accounts like the bank and retirement.

3. **Next, ensure you educate your children on the differences between creating a Will and a Living Trust.** A Will is a legal declaration of a person's wishes regarding the disposition of his or her property or estate after death. A Living Trust is an arrangement in which one or more people manage or take care of the property for someone else's benefit. A Living Trust is created while you are still alive. The title of your property is transferred from your name to that of the Trustee of the Living Trust. Both are useful estate planning documents that serve different purposes, and both can work together to create a complete estate plan.

One main difference between a Will and a Living Trust is that a Will goes into effect only after you die, while a Living Trust takes effect as soon as you create it. A Will directs who will receive your property at your death, and it appoints a legal representative to carry out your wishes. By contrast, a Living Trust can be used to begin distributing property before death, at death, or afterward.

Another difference between a Will and a Living Trust that you need to be aware of is that a Will passes through probate. That means a court oversees the administration of the Will, ensures it is valid, and that the property gets distributed the way the deceased wants. A Living Trust passes outside of probate, so a court does not need to oversee the process, which can save time and money. Unlike a Will, which becomes part of the public record, a Living Trust can remain private.

While I am no expert on the process of establishing a Will or Living Trust, my research has convinced me that both should be a part of your overall plan.

4. **Equally as important, you will need to designate beneficiaries.** A beneficiary is a person you choose to receive your inheritance. That can include but not be limited to your belongings, retirement, and bank accounts. The person or persons will receive all your account balances in the event of your death. Typically, all they will need to do is show a copy of the death certificate and photo identification to the bank.

A person can become a beneficiary without being named, such as in the case if there are children or a spouse. However, you should consider a first and secondary beneficiary to help ease the process after your death.

5. **While you are well, alive, and of sound mind, consider writing out your last wishes.** If you do not know where to start, believe it or not, there are blank templates available online that you can use to take the guesswork out of it for you.

   Your last wishes include things like key details of your funeral service, eulogy notes, how to access accounts, where relevant documents are located, a list of who to call, special thanks, and favorite Bible verses, just to name a few. You can make the list as detailed as you would like. I am sure your loved ones will both appreciate and honor your last wishes.

   A well-prepared plan will also take some of the pressure off your loved ones at such a trying time. Plus, having your last desires spelled out is a bit different from a Will or Living Trust because the document has no legal impact.

6. **Lastly, one of the most important parts of your plan is talking to your children and loved ones about your final arrangements.** A funeral can be expensive these days and, by the time your time here on this earth has

expired, it will be even more costly. Oddly enough, that is a good thing because that means you have lived even longer. The cost usually includes basic fees, optional goods and services, and any special arrangements.

Also, as part of the conversation with your children, you will need to discuss where you would like to be buried or if you would prefer to be cremated. Although difficult, the conversation is necessary.

Being buried in a traditional funeral, which usually consists of a visitation, a funeral or memorial service, and a casketed burial, is probably the most expensive option, so do not rule out other options such as cremation or even donating your body to medical science. The final decision depends on your desires, your loved ones' desires, and how comfortable your family is with carrying out your last wishes.

I had the privilege of attending a funeral planning session with my mother, brothers, and sisters. My mother was alert and knew exactly what she wanted before we talked to the funeral representative. The whole interaction was an eye-opening experience that I will never forget. After the appointment, I quickly realized I needed to start planning my own final arrangements, as I learned there are more options and details than I initially knew. For example, do not forget to let your loved ones know if you are an organ donor. Being a donor can be considered your last act of kindness and is another way to give back to the community because there are thousands of people awaiting life-saving organ transplants.

Regardless of your overall plan, it is a good idea to involve your children and loved ones in the development of that plan. That way, there should be no misunderstanding of your last desires.

I have known people who have written goodbye letters or, as I like to call them, "See You Later Letters." Others have made voice recordings to each of their loved ones. To some, that may seem a little creepy, but it is another way to leave your children a part of you, especially if they are young at the time of your passing. It will be something they will cherish for the rest of their lives.

As my mother has stated many times, her prayer is that *"the family stays together and loves and trusts each other with the love of Jesus as He shows us through His Word."* Going forward, those are words that the family will honor and live.

PARENTING MEMOIR

A Time to Re-Energize

If you have ever flown on an airplane, part of the flight attendant's preflight directions to all passengers is to don your oxygen mask in the event there is an emergency, such as a loss of cabin air pressure or increased turbulence. In addition, if you are going to help others put on their mask (i.e., your children), you are instructed to don your own mask first, then proceed to help others. The order of those procedures is not by chance but has science behind it to back it up. It has been proven that after a few minutes, if your brain goes without oxygen, you start to lose the ability to complete basic cognitive functions. After ten minutes, severe neurological damage generally occurs with no chance of being reversed.

Can you imagine watching your child during an in-flight emergency and not being able to help them properly put on their mask because your brain has a lack of oxygen? That feeling of helplessness will probably cause you to panic even more.

Now, think of being a single parent with the huge responsibility of taking care of your children as the sole breadwinner. You are the only one they count on to provide everything they need and to assist them during emergencies. Therefore, you **must** put on your oxygen mask first before you can be their personal emergency technician. **You must take care of yourself first.**

While we put a lot of time and energy into caring for our children, it is equally as important to take time out for yourself. There are plenty of cost-effective and fun things you can do to help you relax your mind. You can either do things alone or make it a family affair. Getting all the children together to take a short family vacation can seem like a lot of work, so you will have to decide what works best for you and your specific situation. Still, you will eventually need to take time out just for you.

Believe it or not, listening to music while driving is one of the things I do to relax my mind. For many people, driving is a stressful event. It is not that way for me. Often, I sing my favorite songs at the top of my voice, which makes the commute more enjoyable. It does not matter what it sounds like because I am all alone in my car and can adlib all I want. However, I cannot ignore the strange looks from those in other vehicles around me, but I do not allow them to prevent me from auditioning for the next "You've Got Talent" show!

PARENTING MEMOIR

When I take a drive home to Delaware, one of my first stops is Rehoboth Beach. There is something about an early morning walk on the beach that is extremely relaxing, especially before the sun rises. Listening to the waves beat against the shoreline and fishing pier provides healing for the soul as they serve to replace all the negative energy with positive thoughts and affirmations. The sound of the seagulls and the sight of the sun rising over the horizon provides a picture-perfect morning.

During that time, there are no thoughts of appointments, meetings, telephone calls, or deadlines to meet. In that place, only the peace of God and tranquility meet me there.

I am also reminded of an annual drive I take to soak in the picture-perfect view of the Fall foliage in the Shenandoah National Park in Virginia. Autumn not only brings cool, crisp mornings; it also displays vivid, changing colors right before my eyes. There are many shades of highly-defined green, orange, red, brown, and yellow — all magnified by the morning dew against the backdrop of the rising sun and flawless blue sky. (If you have never been to that part of the country, I recommend that you put it on your bucket list of must-see destinations. I promise you will not be disappointed.)

Another thing you can do to ease your mind from the stresses of parenting is to get a massage. I try to treat myself to a massage at least every two months (and more frequently when my schedule allows). There are several benefits to getting a massage, such as reducing stress and muscle tension. You would be surprised at how the muscles tighten from doing basic everyday tasks. Now, add in taking care of children to the mix. Before you know it, other health-related issues can surface, such as headaches, insomnia, and digestive problems. Some of my male friends have stated they have never gotten a massage. I was the first to tell them they do not know what they are missing! Treating yourself to that type of pleasure is good for your mind and body.

Exercising is another fun activity you can do alone or with your children. It will improve your overall mood and help relieve stress, as well. Participating in a regular exercise program or developing a routine can help build strong muscles and bones, increase energy levels, improve the quality of your sleep, and reduce your risk of acquiring chronic conditions like heart disease and high blood pressure. If you decide to include your children and make exercising a family affair, you will see a noticeable difference in their behavior as well. By nature, children usually have lots of energy, so what better way to help them burn off some of that excess than making it fun for the whole family? Jumping rope, bike riding, walking in the park, and bowling are just a few fun-filled activities you can do to get the whole family involved.

With today's use of video games and cell phones, children are often left without getting any exercise outside of the limited amount they get when doing physical education classes at school. That lack of exercise can increase the risk of being overweight, which can lead to child obesity — **a serious problem in the United States.** At the time of this writing, the Center for Disease Control and Prevention quotes obesity rates as high as 25.8% for Hispanics, 22.0% for non-Hispanic Blacks, and 14.1% for non-Hispanic Whites. Regardless of one's race or ethnicity, those rates are way too high. Therefore, we should want to make exercise part of our daily routine.

Another way to help rejuvenate your mind is to create a special, quiet place in your home. It does not have to be a large space, but one where you can simply sit alone to clear your mind. It could be in the corner of a room, under the staircase, in a spare bedroom, or even in a closet. The idea is to set aside that uncluttered area for you to unclutter your mind. With your numerous mandatory daily tasks and busy schedule, you may only be able to spend five or ten minutes in your place of retreat. If that is all you can be afforded, take it! Do not take those few minutes for granted.

Parenting can bring on a tremendous amount of stress and pressure, especially single-parenting. The main idea is to demand and allocate some "me-time" and quiet time to clear your mind. There are many cost-effective ways to re-energize yourself that will not leave you penniless or with additional debt, so be sure to take advantage of them before the situation takes advantage of you.

Depending on the circumstances, you may not always be able to put yourself first. However, with a little careful planning, you will notice a difference. Once you are refreshed and have your oxygen mask tightly secured, it is time to assist your children with their infinite needs and wants.

PARENTING MEMOIR

The School Years

During my son's elementary school years, it was challenging to balance my work requirements and his school requirements. At the time, I was blessed to have a job that allowed me to go into the office early and get off at 2:30 p.m. every day. We were also blessed to have a YMCA afterschool program located in the cafeteria of his school, which made it extremely convenient. Parents with children enrolled in the program and who attended that school were able to drop off their kids at 6:30 a.m. The YMCA provided breakfast (if that was a part of the chosen package) and ensured the children were transferred to their correct class in the morning. Since both were in the same building, the children did not have to contend with going outside in the cold or having to be transported by bus.

The afterschool program provided the children with a light snack, which allowed me not to worry about my son being hungry before I got off work. They also ensured the children did their homework, had constructive group time, and were allowed individual playtime. For years, I made breakfast every morning, packed my son's lunch, and cooked dinner every night. After a long day's work, nothing meant more to me than to see my son's smiling face when I picked him up in the afternoon. Having the YMCA nearby and their afterschool program relieved some of the pressure of being a single father. I am forever grateful they were available.

Since my son had grown into a responsible kid, I allowed him to catch the bus to school when he transitioned to the 4th grade. We lived in a nice one-bedroom apartment with extra space I used for an office. That space was surrounded by a wall of windows. During that time, I would get off work, make it home, have a snack ready, and start dinner by the time the bus dropped of the kids. The arrangement was convenient as well because the bus dropped them off right outside of our first-floor apartment. Sitting in my office, I could see when the bus arrived and would greet my son at the door. Added blessings through it all included my son adapting to his new responsibility, his newfound freedom, and my ability to do my work without the worry of having to make it in time to pick him up from school.

When he transitioned to the 5th grade, he was allowed a little more freedom. I decided to give him a key to the house, just in case I was unavailable or had not made it home from work when the bus dropped the kids off from school. I felt comfortable giving him a key because he had proven himself to be trustworthy and responsible. That action fits the definition of a **"latchkey child,"** which is where children are given a key to the house and allowed to let themselves in without supervision.

Before giving him a key, I conducted a little research to become familiar with state laws. I found that 30 out of the 50 states do not have a minimum age for a child to stay at home alone. The minimum age for 14 out of the 50 states ranges from six to 12 years old. I could not find any data on the minimum age requirements for the remaining six states.

My son's elementary school years brought on new challenges. During that time, I decided to go back to school to obtain my Master's Degree in Business Administration, with a concentration in Human Resources. At first, I was a little skeptical because I was not sure how I was going to work out the schedule. However, after having a talk with God about it, I placed my trust in Him and decided to give it a try.

The school I attended was located on a military base about 15 miles away from home. In order to get my feet wet and get accustomed to my new routine, I enrolled in only one class. I wanted to see if I could handle the school requirements, my work schedule, and home duties as well. The class was held two nights per week: Tuesday and Thursday nights, from 6:00 p.m. to 10:00 p.m. I successfully completed the course, but it was not without its difficulties along the way. By the time I finished class and drove home, it was approximately 10:35 p.m. That was entirely too late for me to ensure my parenting duties were taken care of, which included making sure my son completed his homework, taken his bath, eaten a good meal, and was in bed at a decent hour. I was fortunate enough to find a trusted person who needed extra money and provided babysitting services. That person worked in the rental office of my apartment complex and conveniently lived on the property as well. Therefore, she stayed at my apartment on the nights when I had class, helped my son with his homework, and assisted with preparing him for the next day. Most often, by the time I returned home from class, he was either dozing off to sleep or had already fallen asleep after playing with the sitter's two dogs.

After completing that first semester of late-night commuting to and from class, I decided to explore other options. Hours of research included talking to a few single mothers. I then chose to enroll in an online master's degree program at a local college, which turned out to be a smart move because I could complete all my classes online. In less than two years, I successfully finished my degree!

I will admit that even **that** arrangement came with its own set of challenges, but I stuck to a strict regimen to ensure I had everything covered. For example, after my son was fast asleep, I spent many nights way past midnight doing my homework. While that schedule may not work for everyone, I found that method worked well for my work and single-parenting lifestyle. I could complete assignments and still spend valuable time with my son. Regardless of what I had going on, I ensured he had everything he needed, to include my full attention.

Enter in the middle school years and new challenges. Although the school was close in proximity to our home, the logistics of getting my son to the before- and after-school program posed a different problem. However, I was able to take advantage of the YMCA program once again. During that time, I would drop my son off at the YMCA in the morning. They would transport the children to the appropriate school, pick them up from school, and transport them back to the YMCA afterschool program. The setup was also helpful because it allowed me to continue to work and not worry too much about rushing to pick him up after work.

Unfortunately, the middle school my son attended did not appear to be very accommodating to students who showed any type of learning disability—not to mention they were not well-organized, which drove me batty. I made it a point to stay in constant communication with the front office and the teachers. I also spent a lot of time in parent-teacher conferences—most initiated by me because I wanted to get a firsthand account of some of the things my son told me.

During his 6th- and 7th-grade years, I noticed my son appeared to be more hyper than before at school. He had always been a highly active kid, but the difference was that at home, he could release that growing energy by participating in various outside activities. Of course, one of the first things the school district wanted to do was test kids for Attention-Deficit Hyperactivity Disorder (ADHD), especially boys…and, more specifically, African American boys. As mentioned previously, ADHD is a chronic condition marked by persistent inattention, hyperactivity, and sometimes impulsivity.

I want to bring attention to this disorder because it is very real and something parents should be aware of. I encourage you to learn more about the condition so that you can recognize some of the symptoms.

I did everything I could to ensure my son was doing what he was supposed to do in class, as well as ensure the teachers were doing what they were supposed to do in terms of providing the necessary accommodations.

One of the hardest decisions I had to make during that time was whether to experiment with medication for ADHD. In today's pharmaceutical market, the most common medications prescribed to treat ADHD symptoms are:

- Ritalin
- Concerta
- Metadate
- Adderall
- Dexedrine

While I am not a doctor, I spent many hours researching the list of medications, what they were supposed to do, and their side effects. After weeks of research, I allowed the doctor to prescribe my son one of the medications on the list. However, after approximately three months, I decided to discontinue administering the drug mainly due to the side effects that I witnessed right before my eyes. My son experienced a loss of appetite, loss of weight, and was in a constant zombie-like state. That behavior was the total opposite of the active and happy kid I knew. The **adverse** side effects far outweighed the *proposed* benefits.

The combination of a mediocre middle school and the side effects of the medication was too much for me, so I decided to try something else. I allowed my son to play on the school's football team to help burn off some of his excess energy. From that experience, he was able to attend one of the National Football League player's summer football camps at the University of West Georgia. Although it was a lot of fun, I could tell that playing football was something he did not want to do for more than one season.

The next sports we tried were basketball and recreational soccer leagues at the local YMCA. During those times, all the players seemed to be equally talented, and, at the end of the seasons, each player received a trophy. There were no "winners" or "losers." Out of the three sports my son played, I would say he enjoyed playing basketball the most.

My son and I still kid about one of his fondest memories while playing basketball. His team was down by one point, and he was at the free-throw line. He had a chance to tie or win the game. He was an excellent free-throw shooter and had a good shooting form. I had worked with him on the basics of playing basketball, so I knew he could make the shots. Unfortunately, he missed both shots, and his team lost. After missing both free-throws, he was a little down on himself. I, however, found that to be a great teaching moment for both of us. To this day, we talk about that game from time to time and still have a good laugh about it.

During those middle school years, I decided to ditch the apartment life, buy a house, and move to a new school district. That change was much better for my son in terms of his academics and overall class behavior. I immediately saw a change in him as he came into his own. It turned out that move was a great decision for our family!

The next milestone was his high school years. During most of those years, I took a more hands-off approach as I watched my son grow into a productive young man. At times, it was hard watching him make mistakes, but it was also gratifying watching him discover his hidden talents. As his father, I wanted to make sure he did not make the same mistakes many of his friends made, including some of the same mistakes I made while in high school.

The more I thought about it, the more I realized our family dynamic and living situation was a bit different than any of his friends. I was a working **single father** with a good job who took pride in creating a loving and nourishing family environment. Most of his close friends were being raised by **single mothers** who were working two jobs and doing the best they could to raise one to three male children on their own.

As a good way for my son to get involved in the community, gain self-confidence, network, and interact with others outside of school, I enrolled him in the Beautillion Program that was sponsored by one of the local sororities. It was a four-month program designed to prepare high school juniors and seniors for college and subsequent life. During the program, the participants—known as "Beaux"—were required to attend bi-weekly workshops on topics that included:

- Etiquette
- Fiscal responsibility
- Men's health
- Financial aid
- Career preparation
- Other life-sustaining subjects

At the culmination of the program, the Beaux were presented to their parents, friends, teachers, and other guests at the Beautillion Ball, which was a black-tie gala. One of the Ball requirements for the Beaux was to invite a young lady — known as his "Belle" — to escort him for the evening and dance a waltz. The Beaux also had to perform a few steps with their mothers, which I thought was a nice touch to end the night.

Although my son did not particularly like attending all the workshops (mainly because they interfered with his skateboarding and X-box game time), he got out of his comfort zone, pressed through it, and successfully completed the program. We were extremely proud parents.

Looking back, the only thing I would have changed is that I would have consulted with him before enrolling him in the program.

The ABCs of Life

In recent years, millions of American adults have decided to return to school. Reasons range from but are not limited to:

- ➢ Trying to stay ahead in the competitive workforce
- ➢ Learning new skills
- ➢ Boosting their income and overall earning potential
- ➢ Satisfying that inner drive to keep the mind in marathon shape

Whatever the reason, it can be a win-win outcome when the "student" stays the course.

The Department of Labor has recorded all kinds of statistics in the labor market. For example, they monitor how education (or lack thereof) impacts today's workforce. Data and statistics are sliced and diced in every way you can imagine. Collectively or alone, they can tell a story of both successes and failures in various areas. Depending on which side of the fence you are sitting and your ability to think outside of the box, you may love the outcome of your story, or you may hate it.

Regardless of the numbers, they can shine a bright light on disparities in the system itself.

As an Analyst, I spent years analyzing **tons** of raw logistical data. Depending on the validity of the data, I could display the numbers to tell whatever story I wanted. For those with the unique ability to "read between the lines," it would be apparent that small bits of information were missing. Much like those minute details that are often missed while trying to solve a mystery or crime, when put together, they could help shed some light on the story and complete the picture.

In some instances, facts are either unintentionally or intentionally left out. For example, when it comes to analyzing the connection between the labor market and education, one small detail to consider is the number of times people change jobs in a lifetime or how many people have multiple jobs simultaneously. Again, they are little details but could have a significant impact on the outcome of the story.

The moral of the story here is to either return to school **or** educate yourself on the issues. See how you fit into the story and determine what positive impact you can add to it!

The opportunity to return to school presents itself in many forms. Employers have recognized the importance of educating their workforce and have aided employees by paying a percentage (sometimes 100%) of tuition costs, to include all class material. Sadly, that is one golden opportunity many employees do not take full advantage of.

Think about it: The opportunity can result in a person completing an Associate's, Bachelor's, Master's, or Doctoral Degree! Plus, the best thing about it is that it can be done at little to no cost to the individual. At its absolute worst, the only thing it will cost is a little focus, dedication, and time.

There will always be thousands of reasons you tell yourself why you cannot do it, such as time constraints, procrastination, a lack of self-confidence, or lack of motivation. While those things are easily justified, it all depends on your genuine desire to further both your education and the vision of the future you have for you and your family.

Okay. So, you decided to return to school. You completed high school or obtained your GED, worked diligently to acquire your Associate's, Bachelor's, Master's, and Doctoral degrees—to include the highest certifications available in your field of work. Simultaneously, you may find yourself navigating through life as a single parent. That can be a challenge…and when your **REAL** test begins. You may feel as if the odds of achieving your educational goals are against you or that you are just a random number floating around in a large data set, waiting to be swallowed up by the final statistic. The demands of single-parenting present challenges that will force you to go deep within yourself as you search for answers. You will likely question what you thought you had already mastered, making you feel as if you will need to learn your ABCs all over again.

The 'A' will have you questioning your **"ABILITY"** to function as a single parent. You know what you know, but as real-life situations begin to unfold right before your eyes, you may find yourself second-guessing decisions. If you do not control your thinking, your mind will appear to play tricks on you.

Imagine someone giving you a present, and inside that box was another box…and inside *THAT* box was yet **another** box. For those few minutes of continuously opening boxes, the person who gave you the present is somewhat in control of your mind. You are forced to keep your thinking confined inside that space and routine as you anticipate what is waiting in the next box.

The key is to believe in your abilities and decisions, all while thinking outside of the box when searching for answers.

The 'B' will have you questioning your **"BLESSING."** God already knows and has declared the plans He has for you—plans that include prosperity, hope, and a secure future. The good thing is that God has blessed us with a brain to think for ourselves. As soon as you focus your mind on Him, you will quickly realize your children are a blessing—regardless of how they were conceived. Your children are not a 'mistake.' God used YOU to bring them into this world to further His kingdom.

The 'C' will have you questioning your **"COMMITMENT."** Be honest with yourself here: Even though you love your children to death, you may sometimes experience moments when you feel as if you do not want to "do it anymore." You may aimlessly drift down memory lane to the time when it was just you, and you had no responsibilities. After that brief stint in fantasyland, you are abruptly brought back to reality: You are the one who is responsible for your children who are depending on you. Therefore, stay committed to their overall development, wellbeing, and the building of a family legacy.

PARENTING MEMOIR

The Hard Questions

One way to improve any relationship is to ask and answer hard questions. Whether you are on a first date or doing a simple periodic reality check of yourself, asking questions can help improve communication, open a world of trust, and eliminate a lot of uncertainty. If you are in a relationship or simply trying to get to know someone new, I am sure there are key focus areas such as family, community, and career, that you probably have in mind but may not know how to ask the questions. For the most part, your questions should be thought-provoking. The answers must be extremely important to you, or you would not ask them, correct? While there are usually no right or wrong answers, they can help to gain a better understanding of the other person's perspective.

Equally as important is when you find yourself on the opposite end of the rainbow of questions. Being asked a series of questions out of the blue may catch you off-guard and put you in a defensive stance. Taking a quick pause before answering will give you a moment to gather your thoughts. Depending on the type of question, tone, theme, or subject, you may be able to pick up on small tidbits of information that may help you craft a proper response. Most of the time, there is a reason why you are being asked specific questions, so you may need to slow down, gather your thoughts, and ask for clarification when you are not sure of the other person's motives. The most important thing is to be truthful in your responses.

To better myself, I decided to pose a few hard questions to my children. I call them "hard questions" because not only where they hard to ask, but I will also admit I was not sure if I was prepared for their answers. I asked myself, *"Do I **really** want to know the answers to my questions? Can I even **handle** the truth?"*

As you probably already know, regardless of their age, children can be brutally honest. We must be prepared to hear the uncut truth. After all, the truth will always reveal itself in time…even though it may hurt.

So, once I got up enough nerve to ask my questions, I developed a strategy that included asking my questions in a non-threatening environment. I decided to prep my children by telling them why I would be asking a particular set of questions. I wanted them to feel comfortable, be honest with their responses, and to know there would not be any backlash. As a matter of fact, I encouraged and wanted nothing less than their unfiltered truths.

The burning questions I had were centered on being a father and stepfather. Through their eyes, I wanted to know what I could have done better as a parent and what I could do to improve our relationships moving forward. Asking those questions had the potential to do one of two things:

1. Spark new thoughts and ideas that they never really thought about before, **OR**
2. Resurrect old, ill feelings that were never resolved or discussed with anyone.

Either way, I was determined to get insight into their thoughts.

As the responses rolled in, my heart began to race. Unfortunately, at the time, there was a snowstorm in the area, and the Internet and cable service were awfully slow and sporadic. When the storm finally passed, and the Internet was again fully operational, I sat in front of the computer for about 20 minutes before I opened and read the first and then the second response. (I imagine you may want to know the specific contents of their emails, but I will keep them private for now.)

I braced myself for the unknown and absorbed the words on the screen before me. One thing that stood out was that I could have done a better job communicating with them during their school years, specifically during their 6th- and 7th-grade years. After thinking about it, I agreed wholeheartedly. I distinctly recall being a little stricter during those years because I was driving them toward certain goals. Looking back, I now see those goals were probably more of my goals for them versus their own.

In addition, there was a geographical separation during that time that impacted our communication. While not an excuse, if I had a do-over, increased communication would be one thing I would change, especially during those critical years.

The more I thought about my own life, I gained more confidence and decided to stop letting my thoughts get in the way of clear thinking. I started spending more time with God, asking Him the hard questions (at least they were hard for me to ask). At times, I felt I did not have the right to ask God too many questions or that I was unworthy of His replies.

How in the world did I start thinking that way? Why did I believe it? *Surely, those thoughts did not come from God!*

If you could ask God anything you wanted, what would it be? Might it sound something like this:

"God, where were you when…?"

OR

"God, what will it be like when…?"

In my asking, I determined that no matter what, He is always available and that no question is beyond His capacity to answer. As a matter of fact, He is waiting on all of us to come to Him first—either through His spoken word in the Bible or by directly praying to Him. It all boils down to **communicating** and **believing**.

TERRACE V. WHITE

Father's Day

Have you ever thought about the real meaning of Father's Day? What does fatherhood mean to you? While there is no one or perfect answer, your life experiences and interactions with your own father or father figure will impact your responses to those questions.

In the United States, the celebration of Father's Day began back in the early 1900s as a complement to Mother's Day. That special day of acknowledgment is always on the third Sunday in June.

My early memories of the actual day set aside to celebrate Father's Day is a little fuzzy. Since I did not grow up around my biological father, I do not recall having much thought around a specific day to honor him (or perhaps I did think about it but chose to suppress my feelings). Either way, it was not a day that rose to the top of my list as something I looked forward to celebrating.

As far as my grandfather was concerned—the man and father figure who raised me—every day was Father's Day because we honored him that way. I have many fond and delightful memories of being in his presence. It was a joy to honor him in even the smallest ways. Since we did not have much money back then, he taught and showed me it was the little things that counted, such as small acts of kindness daily.

I remember making sure his slippers were placed at the foot of his favorite chair so he would not have to look for them after a long, hot day in the fields tending to our crops and well-manicured garden. I also made sure the pillow he used to support his back was in the chair after he spent countless hours doing back-breaking work. *I can only imagine how tired he must have been every day…* Although he never complained aloud, I am sure my grandfather had many stories he could have told that would have made me cry and want to give him a big hug.

As I grew older, my thoughts around Father's Day evolved. I often think about "what could have been" with my biological father, leaving me to wonder if I missed anything. I was blessed, however, to have my grandfather, who I called "Daddy." In my mind, I envisioned calling my biological father every year on Father's Day, just to see how he was doing. **In reality,** I have made that call no more than two times over the years. Numerous times, my mother asked if I have talked to my father. When I would reply I hadn't, she would say, *"He's a good* *man. You should stay in touch."* I believed her and have no reason to think he is not a good man.

In late April of 2020, I finally made several attempts to reach my father. He had been on my mind for a few months, so I decided to reach out to him. A few weeks later, we finally had an uninterrupted chance to talk. Things went very well. I must admit that we had one of the **best** conversations I have had with **anyone** in a long time. It was definitely one of the most memorable. During the call, all the previously self-imposed gaps were filled with meaningful dialogue, and the uncharted road quickly turned to the familiar, with a much brighter future. I think we would both agree that it was nothing but God's grace and mercy that brought us to that point after all these years. Our call ended with a heartfelt *"I love you"* — spoken to each other. What father (or son) does not like hearing those three words?

As far as me celebrating the Father's Day holiday, I can honestly say that I celebrate it every single day. To me, fatherhood is one of life's greatest joys. Father's Day is just one joyful day of the year, but the real joy comes the other 364 days of the year as well. Since I consider myself a good father and provider throughout the year, on Father's Day weekend, I find myself smiling a lot at the thought of how my children have grown and become productive citizens in their own unique ways. On that special weekend, I am content with spending time reflecting, thinking about what the next year may bring, and enjoying the fruit of my labor.

Talking to my children on the phone and texting is one thing, but it brings joy to my heart when I see them and can reach out to give hugs. It seems like each time I see them, I notice something different about them. (They have no clue that they are being watched and admired by me.) Often, it is something as small as noticing a mannerism they do that reminds me of myself. Knowing those little secrets melts my heart and makes me smile, as I am a proud father.

Reflecting on the events of my life, I can honestly say I do not have many regrets, if any. Each milestone, major incident, and a sign of mercy was meaningful and purposeful. Some are more memorable than others. However, there may have been a few lost moments…but no *regrets*. Indelible into my memory are those lost moments I often long for with my grandfather. Perhaps back then, I was too young and did not realize the opportunity to create precious moments would not be available forever. Once the opportunity passes, it becomes just a "what if" memory. I cannot redeem any of those lost moments by cashing in on them later in life. Still, the moments

I do vividly remember and carry with me to this day are the ones I cherish the most. I use them to gain strength to get through tough times or to simply be reminded of what a real father should be—not just on the day set aside to celebrate Father's Day, but all day, every day, and every year.

PARENTING MEMOIR

A Call to Serve

I cannot write about my experiences of being a single father without including the second most important time in my life that helped to prepare me for my parenthood journey.

It was a time that began with a lean, shy, wide-eyed kid with a vividly colorful imagination and big, unclear dreams — dreams that often floated away due to the lack of uncertainty or they were overcome by other events.

You see, I have always had a gift to see things in a different light than most people. I not only looked at what was directly in front of me, but I also looked at the opposite as well as the hidden pieces and possibilities. For a while, I thought there was something wrong with my thought process, but as I got older, I realized my heightened senses and God-given gift helped me to analyze and resolve situations quickly.

As a high school junior and senior, I remember sitting in the window of our small three-bedroom house looking at the bright glow in the night (something I did numerous times on Friday nights). Our house was one of three that was newly-built in what I now know as a subdivision. It was always pitch-black outside, except for those lights that shone over the top of the tree line and the sky that was usually filled with millions of stars. It was as if someone had strategically placed the city of Las Vegas in the middle of our little town.

Echoing through the darkness were chirping crickets and the sound of drums. The sound coming from the bass drums had a recognizable, low, and indefinite pitch. The sounds from the snare drums were sharp and more distinctive. Together, they engaged in a long call-and-response conversation that lasted for hours. I often smiled to myself as I bobbed my head to the groove and rhythm of the beats. Those sweet sounds were provided by none other than the Brooks County Marching Trojan Band. Although I was not allowed to attend the football games, my imagination placed me right in the stand at the 50-yard line, chatting it up with my friends each week. Watching those Friday night lights and listening to the drumbeats served to put my imagination into overdrive.

As I sat in the window, I thought of the possibilities that laid on the other side of the tree line and the places they could take me. I was not sure how I would get there, but just thinking about the outside world gave me the drive to pursue a dream of seeing the world.

My dream was further egged on from watching the 1965-1970 television sitcom, "I Dream of Jeannie." The show's main characters were an astronaut (Captain Tony Nelson of the United States Air Force), his best friend and fellow astronaut (Captain Roger Healey of the United States Army Corps of Engineers), and a beautiful "Jeannie" [genie] in a bottle. Their ability to get in and out of unconventional situations unscathed piqued my interest even more and impacted my decision to join the United States Air Force right out of high school.

Growing up in a small town, I was unsure how I would adapt to the possibility of living in larger towns and cities, let alone visiting and living in other countries. However, I was quite confident in my upbringing and the fact that my grandparents had provided a superb foundation. They taught me how to treat others, cook, clean, and love God, so I figured the world had to prepare for me—**versus me preparing for it!**

Back then (in the late '70s), there was no longer a military draft. It was strictly a voluntary force with all branches of the military. During that time, you had to be 18 years old to join, or else your parents or guardian had to sign the paperwork authorizing you to join. My independence would not allow me to ask my grandparents to sign the paperwork, although I am sure they would have gladly done so. Since I would turn 18 years old three weeks after graduation, I decided to wait before I went away to basic training.

Two weeks after turning 18 years old, my dreams started to come into focus. The journey that changed the course of my life began.

My first stop was the Military Entrance Processing Station in Jacksonville, Florida. Depending on where you reside in the United States, that was one of the 65 places all recruits went for testing and medical examinations when entering the military.

Jacksonville was a much larger city than what I was used to, but I was not scared because I was so excited to take my first major step away from home. Walking around downtown Jacksonville and looking at the tall buildings put me in mind of all those Friday nights when I used to sit at the window, waiting for the time my name would be called. I started to think about finally getting the chance to see what was on the other side of the tree line. The streets were busy, and the sidewalks were filled with people from all races and backgrounds.

One day, just as I was about to cross one of the major streets, the reality of city life smacked me in the face. Suddenly, about four or five police cars surrounded me in the middle of the crosswalk! The commotion startled me a bit, but it was more alarming because their cars were so close to me. The officers did not draw their weapons, but they did instruct me to stop and put my hands up. I had watched enough movies and was smart enough to know I needed to comply **immediately**. It turns out there was a suspect who had just robbed a convenience store around the corner, and I fit the description—right down to the same color shirt and pants. After I told them where I was headed and showed them my military papers, they quickly apologized and let me go. The whole incident lasted roughly 20 minutes.

After leaving Jacksonville, my next stop was San Antonio, Texas, which was where all recruits in the Air Force received their initial basic military training. In the late '70s, basic training was six weeks long. Today, the training is 8 ½ weeks long. For the recruits, our day started early in the morning, consisting of a series of strict instructions and bus or airplane rides to get us to our training locations. By design, classes of 25-30 recruits arrived around 9:00 p.m. weekly.

The first thing the Training Instructors did was demand order, respect, discipline, and teamwork. That was accomplished by breaking each of us of all those civilian habits of having a bad attitude and being disrespectful. There were several guys I just knew were not going to make it. They all had a tough guy or bad attitude and were determined not to follow directions. However, after about 30 minutes of continually being screamed at by two or three Training Instructors, they were broken down to their lowest level and soon got with the program. It was easy for me to conform because **none** of the Training Instructors were tougher than my grandmother, with the most significant difference being that she trained me with lots of love. Some time later, I found out the Training Instructors trained in a similar way.

I always paid attention to details and followed instructions very well. That quality did not go unnoticed during the initial stage of training. Therefore, I was selected to be a Squad Leader at the end of week one, which turned out to be my first leadership position. The position was designed for mature recruits with the ability to handle increased responsibilities under pressure. I was responsible for managing 8-10 other recruits, ensuring they did what they were supposed to do. Based on my upbringing and overall mindset, it was an easy job. I treated my teammates with dignity and respect, which allowed us to gel in a short time and be successful.

At the end of those long 12-hour training days, one of the things that got me through each night was a small red three-inch Bible I had purchased at the airport. It was filled with inspirational verses from each chapter of the Bible. Reading those scriptures helped me through stressful situations during training and beyond.

After leaving basic training in San Antonio, my next stop was Denver, Colorado. That was where one of the technical schools was located for basic training graduates to learn the job they would do during their military career. There were also students from the other branches of the military and international students attending training in Denver as well. However, most students were in the Air Force preparing for training in Aerial Photography, Culinary, Finance, Electronics, Intelligence, Missile Guidance, Contracting, and Logistics career fields. There was also an undergraduate Pilot Training Program on the base.

Technical school was a bit different than basic training. Although there was an around-the-clock, three-shift, six-days-a-week training schedule, we had a lot more freedom. I was on the 6:30 a.m. – 12:00 p.m. shift, which left a lot of time to explore the local area. All I had to do was make it back to the base by the 10:00 p.m. curfew and then to class the next morning. During that time, we learned a lot, and life was great!

The next stop for me was overseas to Japan. The base was 28 miles from Tokyo (the country's capital) and had a population of approximately 13 million people. It was during that two-year assignment when I transitioned from an adolescent into a young man with great responsibilities.

I recall questioning my decision to go overseas that very first day in Japan. The language barrier, foods, and unfamiliar sights and sounds played tricks on my mind. However, after the second week, I became a connoisseur of the local cuisine, was more aware of my new surroundings, and appreciated being a true international traveler. As often as possible, I got away from the Americanized local area around the base to explore the Japanese culture and see what the country had to offer.

One of the first self-imposed challenges presented in Japan was to climb Mount Fuji by walking up the hiking trails to the summit. The higher up the mountain I went, the thinner the air got. Since I had just spent time in the high altitude of Denver, Colorado, my lungs and limbs were able to proceed up the steep trails and into the clouds without issue. Once I reached Station 5, I purchased a wooden walking stick as a souvenir and got it stamped, indicating my progress on the path to the summit. I never made it to the summit because the entire walk was a two-day trip. Still, the experience was one I will always remember.

I also went to see one of the ten Buddha statues in Japan, visited several countryside villages and botanical gardens, and frequently rode their rail system, to include the high-speed train. Overall, my stay in Japan was outstanding!

While I was enjoying the experience of a lifetime in a foreign country, I received word that my grandfather passed away on March 25, 1981. The man who taught me everything I knew up until I joined the military was no longer with me. The flight from Japan to the United States is normally about 13 hours nonstop, but on the day of my return, it seemed like 13 days. In between naps, I remember having a numb feeling most of the flight. I could not believe my grandfather was gone. Although there would have been nothing I could have done, I shouldered the burden of blaming myself for not being there when he passed. After all, he had been my father, an example of a real man, and the solid rock of the family all my life. Although I did not get a chance to tell him how much he meant to me, remembering the heartfelt times we spent together gave me the strength to move forward as a young man, even to this day.

After leaving Japan, my next stop was Del Rio, Texas, which had a population of about 32,000 people back in the early '80s. It was a pilot training base out in the middle of nowhere that was located approximately 150 miles West of San Antonio, Texas, but only nine miles from the Mexico border. The city was connected to Ciudad Acuna, Mexico, by the Lake Amistad Dam International Crossing. The base was the biggest employer in the local area, followed by the U.S. Border Patrol. A couple of times per month, we freely walked across into Mexico to do a little shopping and see the lights.

Del Rio was a small town with not much to do for young people. There was only **one** nightspot in town called "The Electric Cowboy." That was where I learned how to do the Cotton-Eyed Joe line dance. I am sure I was a funny sight to see at first, but I eventually got the hang of it. As an escape and a chance to get away from the base, I played on the base's men's basketball team. We traveled all over the states of Texas and Colorado. We were not particularly good in comparison to the other teams, but we had more fun because it was more about the camaraderie than winning at the time.

PARENTING MEMOIR

Time spent in Del Rio was memorable in more ways than one because that is where my daughter was born. I considered myself to be a bright, responsible young man but did not have any experience nor the expertise to raise a child. The only thing I could relate parenting to was the time I spent as a teenager babysitting my little cousins, Patricia and Stacey, many years before. Parenting my **own** child was something on an *entirely* different level. For me, reality kicked in when I saw the ultrasound, heard her heartbeat, and felt the first kick. Each time a new milestone came, it made me realize my life was about to change at the age of 22. I was not sure how much, but I knew the changes would be monumental and everlasting.

At that time, I had almost four years in the U.S. Air Force under my belt and was considering getting out of the military. However, the idea of being a father caused me to have a change of heart. I had the discipline and had always been a responsible person, so the idea of being a father was not too scary (although I must admit that fear did creep into my mind from time to time).

One of the changes I had to work on immediately was the fact that I had always been by myself and was responsible for taking care of only me. Suddenly, I had a delicate and beautiful bundle of joy to care for. I was no longer able to come and go as I pleased. I could no longer do the things I used to do when I wanted to do them. I had an enormous responsibility, another mouth to feed, and someone who would depend on me one way or another for the rest of my time on earth.

After Del Rio, I was on my way to Langley Air Force Base in Hampton, Virginia. Langley was one of the oldest bases in the Air Force and was known for its global deployments and maintaining overall air superiority. The daily pace was focused, fast, and rewarding. My stay there was the real beginning of my fatherhood training.

The move from Texas to Virginia meant I had to find affordable housing and safe daycare. Fortunately, the military does an outstanding job assisting families with transitioning to a new base community. The available resources took the sting and frustration out of settling into a new environment.

While stationed at Langley, I experienced the typical baby/toddler milestones in my daughter's life: teething, crawling, and her first steps. Many sleepless nights included walking around the house in complete darkness while dealing with aching gums, ear infections, and common colds. Nonetheless, I was glad to be a part of the solution to those problems. Thankfully, my job did not take me away too many times during that critical time of my daughter's life. The longest time away was spent in Amsterdam, Holland, for approximately three months (considering the base's mission and compared to other branches of the military, a consecutive three-month stay was not a long time).

When my time was up in Virginia, my next duty station was in Sacramento, California—the state's capital city that sits at the joining of the Sacramento River and the American River. It is known as the "hipster" city and is a major educational hub, filled with museums, financial districts, and historic downtown. Experiencing the west coast style of living was a bit different than that of the east coast I had known all my life. However, after a few weeks of the California sun and laidback way of life, I quickly traded my heavy coats and subdued demeanor for flip-flops, short pants, and a perky attitude.

The primary mission of the base was to train pilots and navigators on various training aircraft. It also had Strategic Wing of Bomber and Refueling type aircraft. The entire Sacramento area was one of the world's best-kept secrets. Unfortunately, the base closed in 1993 due to the Congressional Base Realignment. As a result, a lot of history was transferred to other bases, leaving behind thousands of great memories like playing on the two-time championship men's basketball team—better known around the state of California and the Air Force Air Training Command as the "Mather Air Force Base Skynights." Due to Mather being a training base, the overall day-to-day duties did not appear to be as intense as my previous base in Virginia, although it was equally important.

During that assignment, there was only one extended stay away from my daughter, which was for approximately six weeks to attend a training class in Colorado. The remaining time away was to play in basketball tournaments for two- to three-day periods of time.

After five years at that base, life took a turn. There were rumors that the base was closing. Plus, it was time for me to go. I chose to stay in the area until it was time for me to relocate, which was about a year later. During that year, there were a few challenges that came my way, but nothing got in the way of me seeing and spending time with my daughter. I made that time count, and I am so thankful that I did.

Next, it was off to the Republic of South Korea. That base was located on the west coast of the peninsula near the Kum River. Korea was a different place altogether—more than any of the other bases I had previously been assigned. It was extraordinarily cold during the Winter months and hot and steamy during the Spring and Summer months. Since the assignment was for only one year, I figured I would make the best of it. Our teams worked hard, accomplished a lot, played hard, laughed a lot, and I made lifelong friends. That year flew by extremely fast.

Glendale, Arizona, was my next stop—approximately 10 miles west of downtown Phoenix. That was also a pilot training base where pilots trained on the F-15 and F-16 fighter aircraft during the time I spent there. Today, those aircraft have been reassigned to other bases, and they were replaced with one of the Air Force's newest: The F-35A.

Overall, being in Arizona was great. Once I learned how to deal with and survive the heat, mesmerizing summer light storms, and occasional haboobs (thick sand and dust storms), my stay in the "Valley of the Sun" was a lot more enjoyable. The Phoenix area has all the major professional sports and all that comes along with the luxury experience, including great food and people, scenic mountains with a picture-perfect sunset as the backdrop, and an experience with the Indian culture that I will never forget. I was surprised to see fields of roses in all colors and to learn that cotton was a part of the local farming community. In addition, if the sun became too much to bear, I could drive two hours north of Phoenix, stop in Sedona to observe the awesome orange and red stone formations, and experience snow in Flagstaff.

The best thing about my time in Arizona was the birth of my son. Being on a training base and having the type of job I had, there was not a requirement from that base for temporary duty assignments that would have taken the average military service member to places like Saudi Arabia in support of Operation Desert Storm during that time. The closest I got to that war was temporary duty in Turkey for four months in support of the war in Iraq, which was over 100 miles away. At the base in Turkey, the conditions of living in a tent were not too bad because the Air Force provided as many comfort items as possible to make things feel more like home. The daily pace was fast and dynamic, which made the time go by fast.

Those four months spent in Turkey was the first time I had been away from my son for more than two nights in a row. I wanted my face to be the first one he saw in the morning when he opened his eyes and the last he saw before he shut down for the night. I wanted to be the protector, provider, and go-to person if he needed anything. During my time away, I called and spoke to him as often as possible. I also sent cards and letters, just to let him know I was thinking about him. At the time, he was less than a year old, so I was not sure how he would react to my absence or if he even realized who I was on the other end of the phone. Nonetheless, I did not let that stop me from calling and sending cards and letters that likely bombarded the U.S. Postal Service regularly.

When I returned home from my trip, I was greeted with balloons, the biggest smile, and the tightest hug I could ever want. To me, it was a true hero's welcome and one I will always treasure. I am not ashamed to admit I got a little choked up by the genuine love I felt between a father and son. From that day forward, there was **no doubt** in my mind that he and I had an unbreakable bond — one that remains strong to this very day.

When I left Arizona, my next base was the beautiful Sicily, Italy. That was a two-year special-duty assignment to a Navy base on the largest island in the Mediterranean Sea, just south of the main Italian Peninsula. Sicily has a rich and unique culture, including its people, art, food, architecture, and history. The weather was great, which helped to produce an abundant amount of wheat, oranges, olives, grapes, almonds, lemons, tomatoes, and, of course, wine. The farmers raised mostly cattle and sheep. There was also a hybrid of a goat and a sheep (affectionately known as "geep"). I often saw them crossing the road within arms-length from my car.

My apartment was in Motta Sant'Anastasia and sat on a hillside overlooking a valley. In the distance was a picture-perfect view of Mount Edna (one of the world's most active volcanos). As a matter of fact, during the day, I could observe the black smoke billowing from the top. At night, the dark sky was illuminated by the red lava flowing from the peak of the mountain. During the Spring and Summer months, I would sit on my balcony at night for hours, staring at the lava show and listening to its resounding rumbling. One might think it would be scary, but for me, it was peaceful and a wonder to see and hear.

One of the most memorable times watching the small volcanic eruptions at night occurred during a George Benson concert in the nearby Amphitheatre of Catania, the capital of Sicily. That night, the moon was full, the sky was filled with stars, and the night air was crisp. The crowd swayed back and forth to the jazz music as volcanic eruptions put on their own show behind the stage. It was *truly* a sight to see and a night to remember.

My assignment to Sicily took me to many other places in northern Italy on the mainland. I also had stints in Germany, England, Turkey, Austria, Belgium, and the Netherlands during that time. The demands of the job were the most stressful I had experienced my entire career, but by far, the assignment was the most rewarding because of the work experience I gained and my team's accomplishments.

The work hours were long, but the off-duty time and weekend journeys allowed me to slow my thinking by meditating, exercising, and spending a lot of quality quiet time with God. It was during those two years that I obtained clear directions and a lot of clarity on life issues. While I missed my children tremendously, the time away was well spent and exactly what I needed to regain my footing. Being away from the daily comforts I was used to in the United States made me appreciate the little things in life even more and made me a more focused, driven, and peaceful person...*and a better father.*

After traveling around Europe for two years, I returned to Virginia—and the hustle and grind of life in the good old United States. I was at peace and focused on what life had to offer. Upon my return, it did not take long to figure out that military career was about to come to an end. I wanted even more out of life and did not want to leave any stones unturned, so after ten short months of being in Hampton, Virginia, for the second time in my career, I made a command decision to make that my last military assignment and retire from the U.S. Air Force. To be honest, my exit plan was a bit shaky, but after spending a lot of time talking and listening to God and putting all my trust in Him, my plan quickly began to take shape. I trusted my new solid foundation and prepared to move forward with the next phase of life with my children.

In answering the nation's highest call to serve my country, I transitioned from a young, wide-eyed boy into an Airman, a man, and a father. For 20 years and 11 months, I served honorably with dignity and excellence, always putting service before self. It was not always easy—especially when I had to leave my loved ones behind—but I learned valuable lessons on how to follow, lead, and inspire others. I have traveled the world, seen some of its best (and worst) places, and met many outstanding people from all walks of life. Through it all, I was made a better man, a better friend, and a better father.

Just as I answered the call to serve this great nation, I continue to answer the call to serve as a father and a father figure. Unlike serving in the military, parenthood has no term limit, no reenlistment bonus, and no leave of absence. However, there is a relentless commitment and dedication to be the best father I can be, leaving no child behind.

I am not afraid. I will not fail, for I know that God did not give me a spirit of fear.

PARENTING MEMOIR

My "Transitions"

Age 2

Age 17

Age 18

Age 37

PARENTING MEMOIR

Child Support

Normally, when parents divorce or the custodial parent or guardian seeks financial support to provide for the children, they go through the state's court system to begin the process. Each state sets its own payment guidelines and may vary in the formulas used to calculate the amount of support to be paid. For example, in California, the amount is based on factors such as the gross income of each parent, the percentage of time each parent spends with each child, available tax deductions, childcare costs, and the tax status of each parent. The payment calculations are complex, so the California court system uses a software program called "Dissomaster."

The state of Virginia uses *similar* calculations but does not use the same software program. Also, most child support programs are managed by a special office, such as the Division of Child Support Services or the Child Support Enforcement Division. They are responsible for monitoring and assisting with collecting payments. The payments may be enforced through withholding the predetermined amount from paychecks or other benefits, as well as from federal and state income tax refunds and lottery winnings. If child support is not consistently paid by the noncustodial parent, the case will be forwarded to the three credit bureaus and to the Department of Motor Vehicles to suspend or revoke driving privileges. In addition, bank accounts, passports, and personal property can be seized.

Regardless of the amount of child support payments mandated by the state, it is imperative to realize the dollar amount is not nearly as important as the physical and mental support your children need. Depending on the circumstances, state laws allow for periodic adjustments to the amount of child support. For example, judges have the power to increase or decrease the award if justified, such as in the cases of obligations to children from another relationship, special needs, or other expenses required by the child. No matter the reason for the adjustment, that does not relieve the noncustodial parent of their duties and responsibilities to be a part of their children's lives, if possible.

Each state typically has a robust program to crack down on child support evaders and to monitor "deadbeat" parents. The word "deadbeat" was adopted in the 1890s and was used to identify a person as a *"worthless, spongy idler."* In order to have a name pop up on a state's "Deadbeat Dad" or "Deadbeat

Mom" website, they must have a court-issued warrant and be at least $5,000.00 delinquent in child support payments. Each website posts the amount owed, along with a photo of the parent who owes the payment.

For this portion of the book, I researched the websites of 17 different states. The delinquent amounts ranged from $5,000.00 up to $745,000.00, with the latter being somewhat of a head-scratcher for me. The sites had **over** 450 pictures posted of deadbeat parents that consisted of approximately 90% men and 10% women of all ages.

In my humble opinion, that is one area where each state needs to make additional investments in collecting those outstanding payments. They should also include it as one of their top focus areas.

You may be wondering, *"Why in the world is he talking about* ***child support?"*** Well, child support is a payment meant to be used for the daily needs of the children, such as food, housing, medical expenses, and recreational activities. However, far too often, child support payments drive a wedge between the custodial and noncustodial parents. Besides being irresponsible and thoughtless of both parents, one of the unintended consequences is that it can drive a wedge between one of the parents and children, which is not good at all. Both parents should do all they can to come to a workable agreement for all parties involved. With that said, I do realize you may not have the luxury of choosing your own agreement, especially if you go through the court system.

Sometimes, the family dynamic is such that one parent is required to pay child support for a child from a previous relationship. If so, that would be one thing that needs to be discussed in detail—and the sooner, the better. A good time to address that issue is when you are talking about your assets, liabilities, and responsibilities. After all, that is money out of your new family's budget. Always keep in mind it is not the child's fault and that the added funds are supposed to take care of the child's needs—not the *parent's* expensive habits.

Lastly, if you are the custodial parent who receives the child support, I would not recommend factoring the support payment to offset your overall living expenses. The reason why is because the amount can be changed (either up or down) at any time by the courts. Plus, you will not receive child support forever, so use it for its intended purpose and use it wisely.

Child support means much more than meeting a financial obligation. It also means supporting your children mentally and spiritually, as well as doing what you say you are going to do on time. I have seen firsthand and heard of instances when a parent promises to do something with their child, only to be a no-show repeat offender. That lack of caring and irresponsibility can be ***devastating*** to a child. At a minimum, a phone call or even a text message explaining the letdown goes a long way in keeping the line of communication open.

There is nothing like having a child wait on the porch or constantly look out the window, waiting for a parent to follow through on a promise. After numerous failed attempts, the child often gives up and may even shut down or want to end all communication. When that happens, the custodial parent should not make excuses for the noncustodial parent. Be honest with your children about the circumstances, and keep a positive attitude. Children who experience those types of instances often carry those memories and weight around for years and years. Time lost can be an expensive cost in more ways than one, and you cannot get that time back.

I recognize that not all circumstances are the same. I do, however, thank God that it never crossed my mind to put my children through that kind of misery.

Statistics show that noncustodial mothers have a lower number of child support agreements in place when the father is the custodial parent. On the surface, that seems like a terrible statistic, but you must wonder why it is that way. After a little digging, I found the **main** reason is that the mother typically makes less money than the father, thereby impacting the amount of child support paid (if there is even an agreement in place). Unfortunately, another reason I found is that the custodial father often decides he does not **need** the support from the mother. That denial could be tied to a negative relationship between the father and mother, or the father does, in fact, make more money and has opted to support the child on his own. In either case, it negatively impacts the child in the end.

In the grand scheme of things, you will not get an award for taking care of your basic parenting responsibilities or financial support you provide. After all, an award is usually given to a person to mark the recognition of a specific achievement.

In August of 2008, I was awarded the Gene Akers Father of the Year Award by the Henrico County Department of Social Services Fatherhood Initiative. The award is named after Lincoln Eugene Akers, a U.S. Navy veteran of WWII and the

Korean War. He received the first Father of the Year Award in Henrico County, Virginia, and afterward, the award was named after him.

To qualify, the nominee had to be a biological father, stepfather, or father role model who demonstrated exemplary dedication and active participation in developing and maintaining a healthy relationship with his family. He had to accept his duty as a father with clear purpose and love, be at least 18 years old, and serve as an excellent image for his children to follow on their journey towards adulthood. The nominees were judged on sustained commitment and evidence of personal sacrifice to his family.

After reading the requirements for the award, I thought, **"Yes, that sounds just like me and the things I do daily!"** For starters, I filled the roles of being a biological father, stepfather, **AND** father role model. I always believed that being a parent is a big part of my calling, and I take the job seriously. I was never one to "toot my own horn," but I felt my dedication and commitment fit the bill for the award. Therefore, I submitted a narrative that highlighted the work I had put in over the years as a single father. To be honest, I was satisfied with the fact that I was bold enough to share a small piece of my daily life with strangers.

As mentioned, I was selected for the award that year. As time went on, I started to think about just how much of an honor it was to be recognized and given such a prestigious award.

Being a loving and supportive parent is much more than a one-time specific achievement. It is a **LIFETIME** commitment and achievement.

PARENTING MEMOIR

"The Talk"

You may have heard many parents say they gave their kids "the talk." Years ago, "the talk" was automatically thought to be a discussion about sex and pregnancy. However, real events have forced parents to expand their "talk" agenda. If parents are to be the change and prepare their children for a change, they must be aware of the latest traps and pressures children face and be ready to take advantage of every opportunity to have "the talk" with them.

Regardless of the subject or how uncomfortable it may be, approaching them first instead of waiting for them to approach you is a viable option. **But wait!** Before you approach them, make sure you have done your homework. Most kids these days know more about what is going on in their immediate surroundings than you do. Do not be surprised if they tell you a few things that would have been unspeakable when you were growing up.

Parents over 35 years old were probably not exposed to the things that today's children are subjected to, beginning as early as elementary and middle school. We used to think drugs, sex, and rock and roll were for adults only. Not so fast, parent!

I recall hearing a few eye-raising stories that occurred at my son's elementary school and afterschool program that made me pay closer attention—activities that were immediately reported to the proper authorities.

From that point on, I began to ask my son more and more questions. I especially wanted to know if he had witnessed or been involved in any tricky situations that would not meet my approval. Moreover, I wanted to make sure he understood my expectations and values and that he should always remain respectful to others and himself.

One thing I did not do was rush through our conversations. Each talk occurred in a nonthreatening environment. Even when there were no conversations, I paid close attention and kept my ears open for an opportunity to talk.

Regardless of how attentive you are and how tight of a ship you think you run at home, some things may slip through the cracks and remain left unsaid. Let us face it: Your children are not going to tell you everything or every little detail about what goes on in the daily activities. If I were a kid, I probably would not tell everything either. The key is to keep the line of communication open so they can express themselves freely.

The explosion of social media has added new challenges and makes direct one-on-one communication a constant battle. An enormous amount of information can be discreetly accessed from your children's mobile devices and computers. Although parental controls are used as a monitoring tool, many children are savvy enough these days and can easily get around established restrictions. Plus, the gadgets and technology are so technical, parents often rely on their children to actually troubleshoot their computers and other smart devices.

One thing **all** parents should try to keep an eye on is bullying, especially on social media. Sometimes, the negative effects of cyber-bullying are not fully known or found out until it is too late. Some of the most dangerous effects of cyber-bullying include:

- ➢ Isolation
- ➢ Low self-esteem
- ➢ Poor concentration
- ➢ Depression
- ➢ Loss of appetite
- ➢ Suicide

Therefore, try to pay attention. Do your homework, but do not overreact. Give children a chance to work through situations and figure things out before you step in. However, ensure you keep a watchful eye on them, just in case things start to deteriorate.

"The talk" can also include any advice you think your children need.

Since I am now in the final quarter of my full-time working years and my children are either just starting out or midway through their careers, I try to give as much sound career advice as possible. Teaching them how to deal with various situations and people on the job is one of my favorite topics to discuss. Early in a conversation or after several conversations, I can usually tell what they are interested in or help them to identify their true passion. I stress the importance of being confident in their abilities and not to be so afraid that fear hinders their growth and progress. That may sound easier said than done, but they must always remember they are never alone, can ask for advice, and should remain resilient in adverse situations.

Today, you cannot have "the talk" with your children without including conversations about what to do when approached by an authoritative figure—something especially useful to have in the "toolbox" if you or your child are an African American male.

Dating back as far as my childhood, I remember being told by my grandfather how to act, to always be respectful, and to keep to myself. At first, I did not understand why he shared those tidbits of information, but as events unfolded right before my eyes, those conversations made sense. I was conditioned not to act up or act out in the presence of authority, especially a grown-up or the police. If, by chance, I decided to go another route besides what I was told, I knew it would not be a pretty conversation between my grandfather and me. Plus, I never wanted to disappoint him. In the presence of the police, I felt comfortable because I always tried to abide by the rules or at least ensure I had a good understanding of the rules. Moreover, I was used to my grandmother's rules, so dealing with the police was easy. If her rules were broken, I could easily find myself on her bad side for a couple of days…*and I did not want that.*

The need for "the talk" has always been there, dating back to the days of slavery, the peak of the Civil Rights Movement in the '60s, and now, the Black Lives Matter movement we have today. While we have made strides toward real equality, we have a long way to go. With the increase in the number of police shootings across the United States, "the talk" with your children—*especially our males*—is needed more and more. There are many statistics to support the increase, but doesn't it make you wonder if the statistics include **all** police shooting incidents? After all, statistical data is partly based on **voluntary** reporting by the various agencies. Not only are there disparities in the numbers related to police shootings, but there are also disparities in the police's use of force, police convictions, and disproportions in the number of incidents by race.

While I cannot be with my son 24 hours a day, our "talks" consist of tips and survival rules to remember when interacting with the authorities, especially the police. For example, I tell him to:

- Be respectful.
- Keep his cool.
- Watch what he says because it can be used against him.
- Be very observant of who is around him and their conversations.
- Keep his hands in plain sight at all times.
- Do not make any sudden moves.
- Whatever he does, **DO NOT RUN!**

PARENTING MEMOIR

Regardless of the circumstances or who is right or wrong, safety comes first. As a family, we can talk about and get through the specific details later. The most important thing is that your children make it home alive!

On a beautiful, sunny Saturday afternoon in mid-April of 2020, my son was stopped by the city police while riding his bicycle in downtown Richmond, Virginia. The officers told him to get off the bike, immediately placed him in handcuffs, and **then** asked for his identification before making him sit on the sidewalk. **Yes, it happened in *THAT* order!** When he asked them why, one of the officers replied, *"You fit the description of an armed robbery suspect."* Apparently, an armed robbery had taken place on Wednesday around 3:00 p.m. that same week. Fortunately, my son was at work during that time, so he had an alibi. After proving to the officers that he was at work on that day **and** at that time, they released him without further incident.

Needless to say, my son was extremely upset and told me he felt helpless. After he shared the story with me within the same hour of the incident's occurrence, I felt somewhat helpless as a father. The good thing was that he remembered the many "talks" we had about staying calm and being as respectful as possible. I realize being cool, calm, and collected during those types of situations is easier said than done, even for a seasoned adult male—especially when innocent. However, things could have easily gotten out of hand over a misidentification.

My mind then began to race with thoughts.

*Was there **really** an armed robbery in the area the same week, and my son "just so happened" to fit the description?*

*Did the police stop him because of the **color** of his **skin**?*

*Was it protocol to put handcuffs on a person and **then** ask for identification?*

In my mind, things did not add up. I immediately conducted an Internet search to determine how to file a formal complaint with the city police chief. Unfortunately, my son did not get the officers' names or badge numbers.

I decided to use the incident as another teaching moment. We went over everything a second time in detail. I gave him pointers on what to look for if a similar event ever happened again. I also shared with him my experience with the police that happened about 40 years earlier in Jacksonville, Florida—which also *"just so happened"* to be a case of mistaken identity of a black male robbery suspect.

PARENTING MEMOIR

What is unfortunate is that there are **still** too many Black and Brown male incidents with the police where the victims are stopped and frisked for no apparent reason other than the police officer's suspicion and word. While I cannot protect my son 24 hours a day, as a father, I can and will stay prayed up for his safety.

TERRACE V. WHITE

Understand Me
© 2020 Terrace V. White

You don't understand me.

Instead of shaking my hands, you cuff my hands

behind my back, as I clutch my hands.

Stop piercing my empty hands

and wipe the blood from your hands.

Eyes wide shut as you refuse

to see what I made with my hands.

Therefore, I extend my hands

and offer a cool drink from the cup in my hands.

Together we can raise our hands

to fervently pray for the other man.

Only then will you begin to understand,

Me!

The last important "talk" to have with your children is about God. I know, I know. It may be a touchy subject in some households, but I believe it is one that must be continually discussed, especially if you are a believer. I guarantee that if you bring it up from time to time as well as pray about it, the right words will be revealed to you at the right time.

It is not your job to solve your children's problems, but it is your job to guide them. What better way to help them navigate through life's situations than to start with a solid foundation built on truth?

To speak the truth, you must first believe it. Once you discover and apply it to your own life, you can begin to share your successes and failures, along with how you overcame various situations. When discussing your life with your children, do not hold back. **Remember:** As much as they may think you are perfect and have it all together, no one is perfect. They should know that by you being open and honest. However, a word of advice here is to not preach to them in such a way that it turns them completely off. While the circumstances may be similar to the ones you have experienced, this generation's thinking is much different than yours. They are more sensitive and may require you to be savvy in how you reach them with your message.

In addition, you must follow your own advice. Do not be self-righteous because if you do, that is a sure way to cloud the communication lines between you and your children. Therefore, be creative with your approach.

Besides "the talks," some of the other things that work for my family include sending daily encouraging scriptures via text message and email and, of course, daily prayer. I usually try to find scriptures that will help them deal with current situations in their life or current events of the day.

You would be surprised at how much those inspirational messages can make a difference in your children's lives. Do not worry about paraphrasing or explaining them too much. Just send them as they are written. Let the Holy Spirit take the lead and leave everything to God. If you cannot find the right words to say for the right situation, maybe it is time for you to have "the talk" with God.

Final Thoughts

Throughout the rollercoaster ride of our time here on this earth, we experience many ups and downs, peaks and valleys, twists and turns, and successes and losses. One thing that remains constant is the joy of parenting. God chose and gave us the responsibility of caring for another precious life that will eventually carry on our legacy.

Most often, our children are the **spitting** image of their parents, in both body and spirit. For me, my children soften my heart and fill it with joy, love, and laughter. They continue to be one of the high points of my life. I celebrate, I cry, I see them at their best, and I watch them grow. I see their strengths, weaknesses, innocence, imperfections, and fears. Through it all, they bring out the best in me in their individual and unique ways.

Effective parenting is a big responsibility, whether you are a single parent or co-parenting. There are many proven and successful parenting tips, but there is no one correct way to parent. Therefore, adapt your style to get the best outcome for your family.

The things shared in this book may seem minor because of the magnitude of your current situation. I can relate to your plight because more times than I care to remember, I found myself trying to **do** all things and **be** all things, which is exhausting. Children force you to show unconditional love on a continuous basis because that is precisely what they give. There are times when they will become the teacher, and you will become the pupil.

Each day is a new frontier…*a new beginning.* Regardless of the events of yesterday, look forward to today's opportunities. Tomorrow will bring new joys and another level of love and laughter.

It has been a pleasure sharing a part of my life and heart as a single father. May God continue to comfort and bless you and your children.

Enjoy the journey!

About the Author

Terrace V. White is a Richmond, Virginia-based first-time author of the nonfictional book, *Parenting Memoir: From the Heart of a Single Father*. After living his childhood dream of serving this country, he retired from the United States Air Force after 21 years of honorable service.

In the next phase of his dream, he found himself in the leading role as a single father, which he welcomed and accepted with honor. In this role, he is:

- The head of the household.
- A provider and educator.
- A spiritual and financial advisor.
- The lone disciplinarian and number one encourager.
- A protector and nurturer.
- The lead instructor and student of the world, and
- A data analyzer and leader by example…just to name a few.

Most of all, he is a dedicated and loving father to his children!

TERRACE V. WHITE

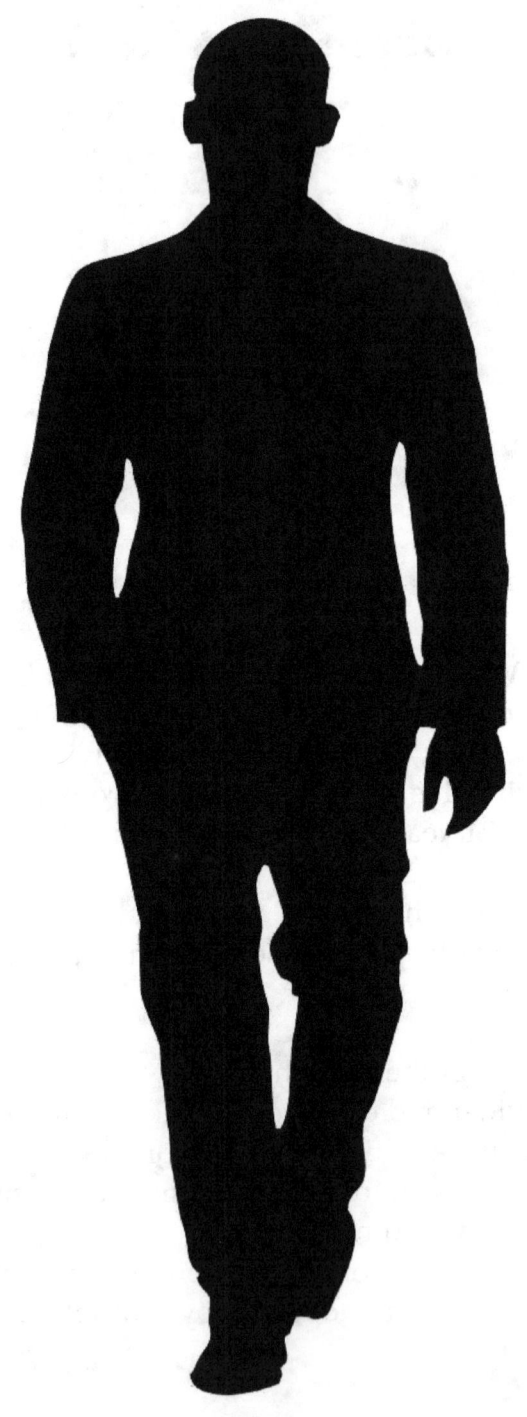

Appendix

1. Habakkuk 2:2. *Then the Lord answered me and said: "Write the vision And make it plain on tablets, That he may run who reads it.*

2. Grall, Timothy. (January 2020). Retrieved from https://www.census.gov/content/dam/Census/library/publications/2020/demo/p60-262.pdf. According to the Custodial Mothers and Fathers and Their Child Support report released by the U.S. Census Bureau, there were approximately 13.6 million single or custodial parents in the United States in 2016, and those parents are responsible for raising 22.4 million children.

3. Mothers Who Leave Their Children. (February 22, 2020). Retrieved from https://www.steadyhealth.com/topics/mothers-who-leave-their-children

4. Population of Quitman, GA. (February 22, 2020). Retrieved from https://population.us/ga/quitman/. This was in the late 70s, down in the deep South, in a small town with a population of about 5,100 people, which was made up of 60% African American, 32% White, and the Other category was made up of Native Americans, Asians, and Hispanics.

5. Deuteronomy 31:6. *Be strong and of good courage, do not fear nor be afraid of them; for the Lord your God, He is the One who goes with you. He will not leave you nor forsake you.*

6. Isaiah 41:10. *Fear not, I am with you; Be not dismayed, for I am your God. I will strengthen you; I will uphold you with My righteous right hand.*

7.   Proverbs 3:5-6. *Trust in the Lord with all your heart And lean not on your own understanding; In all your ways acknowledge Him, And He shall direct your paths.*

8.   Philippians 4:6-7. *Be anxious for nothing, but in everything by prayer and supplication, with thanksgiving, let your requests be made known to God. And the peace of God, which surpasses all understanding, will guard your hearts and minds through Christ Jesus.*

9.   Philippians 4:13. *I can do all things through Christ who strengthens me.*

10.   II Timothy 1:7. *For God has not given us a spirit of fear, but of power and of love and of a sound mind.*

11.   Bradley, B. T. (2019). *Kale Yeah, It's Good…No Meat Necessary (Volume 2).* Pearly Gates Publishing.

12.   Bradley, B. T. (2015). *The 21-Day Vegan Challenge.* Pearly Gates Publishing.

13.   *Demographic Characteristics of COVID-19 Cases in the U.S.* (April 19, 2020). Retrieved from https://www.cdc.gov/coronavirus/2019-ncov/cases-updates/cases-in-us.html.

14.   Matthew 6:33. *But seek first his kingdom and his righteousness, and all these things will be given to you as well.*

15.   Proverbs 16:3. *Commit your works to the Lord, And your thoughts will be established.*

16.   2 Timothy 1:7. *For God hath not given us the spirit of fear; but of power, and of love, and of a sound mind.*

17.   Habakkuk 2:2. *Then the Lord answered me and said: Write the vision, And make it plain on tablets, That he may run who reads it.*

18.   *Childhood Obesity Facts.* (February 22, 2020). Retrieved from https://www.cdc.gov/obesity/data/childhood.html. This lack of exercise can increase the risk of being overweight or child obesity, which is a serious problem in the United States. At the time of this writing, the Center for Disease Control and Prevention obesity rates quoted as high as 25.8% for Hispanics, 22.0% for non-Hispanic blacks, and 14.1% for non-Hispanic whites.

19.   *Data and Statistics About ADHD.* (March 29, 2020). Retrieved from https://www.cdc.gov/ncbddd/adhd/data.html. The Center for Disease Control and Prevention estimates that the number of children ever diagnosed with ADHD, according to a national 2016 parent survey is 6.1 million, with the majority being children aged 6-11 years old.

TERRACE V. WHITE

www.ingramcontent.com/pod-product-compliance
Lightning Source LLC
Chambersburg PA
CBHW072001110526
44592CB00012B/1162